SUPERREADING
for Success

SUPERREADING
for Success

· ·

The Groundbreaking,

Brain-Based Program to Improve

Your Speed, Enhance Your Memory,

and Increase Your Success

RON COLE

JEREMY P. TARCHER

a member of Penguin Group (USA) Inc.

New York

JEREMY P. TARCHER/PENGUIN
Published by the Penguin Group
Penguin Group (USA) Inc., 375 Hudson Street, New York, New York 10014, USA •
Penguin Group (Canada), 90 Eglinton Avenue East, Suite 700, Toronto, Ontario M4P 2Y3,
Canada (a division of Pearson Penguin Canada Inc.) • Penguin Books Ltd, 80 Strand,
London WC2R 0RL, England • Penguin Ireland, 25 St Stephen's Green, Dublin 2, Ireland
(a division of Penguin Books Ltd) • Penguin Group (Australia), 250 Camberwell Road,
Camberwell, Victoria 3124, Australia (a division of Pearson Australia Group Pty Ltd) •
Penguin Books India Pvt Ltd, 11 Community Centre, Panchsheel Park, New Delhi–110 017,
India • Penguin Group (NZ), 67 Apollo Drive, Rosedale, North Shore 0632, New Zealand
(a division of Pearson New Zealand Ltd) • Penguin Books (South Africa) (Pty) Ltd,
24 Sturdee Avenue, Rosebank, Johannesburg 2196, South Africa

Penguin Books Ltd, Registered Offices:
80 Strand, London WC2R 0RL, England

Originally published in the United Kingdom as
How to Be a Super Reader by Piatkus in 2009
First American edition published by Tarcher/Penguin in 2012
Copyright © 2009 by Ron Cole

Most Tarcher/Penguin books are available at special quantity
discounts for bulk purchase for sales promotions, premiums,
fund-raising, and educational needs. Special books or book excerpts also can be created to fit
specific needs. For details, write Penguin Group (USA) Inc. Special Markets,
375 Hudson Street, New York, NY 10014.

ISBN 978-0-399-16043-1

Printed in the United States of America
1   3   5   7   9   10   8   6   4   2

While the author has made every effort to provide accurate telephone numbers, Internet
addresses, and other contact information at the time of publication, neither the publisher nor
the author assumes any responsibility for errors, or for changes that occur after publication.
Further, the publisher does not have any control over and does not assume any responsibility for
author or third-party websites or their content.

Contents

Acknowledgments

In mostly chronological order, I wish to thank:

The Roman scholars who came up with the concept of "the room."

Evelyn Wood for getting the ball rolling with speed reading.

Shanna McBain for putting in a good word for me at Hewlett-Packard.

Mariam Ghazvini for giving the course a chance at Hewlett-Packard, and championing it through the lean years.

Judy Peterson, whose continued enthusiasm at Xilinx was brilliant.

Bonita Steers for suggesting that the testing could be improved.

Reto Stamm for making Eye-Hop™ accessible to everyone.

Jackson Chow for continuing to support SuperReading™ for students.

Claire de Than for her steadfast belief in the project and her desire to help her law students.

Dr. Ross Cooper for his support and professionalism in evaluating the SuperReading™ course for dyslexics, and spurring great ideas for improving the testing procedure.

Don Schloss for promoting SuperReading™ among the dyslexic population.

Doreen Montgomery for finding a super publisher.

Anne Lawrance for believing in SuperReading™ and fully supporting this project.

Carol Franklin for brilliant editing and determining the best order of topics.

All the educators and decision makers who approved SuperReading™ to be taught.

All my students for taking a chance, giving it a go, and proving time and again that the techniques work.

PART ONE:

Starting Out

1.

The lowdown on SuperReading™

There are probably several reasons why you want to be a "super" reader. You may have stacks of reports you need to get through, you may be drowning in e-mails, you may be studying for exams or you may have problems keeping focused. Whatever your reasons are for buying this book, my goal is to help you become a highly effective, confident reader. If you work your way through the advice in this book you will learn how to understand what you read and remember what you need.

In simple terms, you will be able to handle any reading "assignment" that comes your way intelligently, enthusiastically and efficiently. In the days and weeks ahead you will change your attitude toward reading. Whether you love reading or you dread it, your improved skills will make reading something you will always look forward to. Also, you will learn how to use memory tools that will help you retain any information for as long as you wish.

If reading is a chore for you, take heart. Just a couple

of days after picking up this book you will already be reading better. It has been written in a conversational and humorous tone, as if I'm talking to you. If you can simply invest a little time each day, I promise you that your abilities will quickly improve.

What's the SuperReading™ story?

This book is based on the highly successful SuperReading™ course that I have been teaching for over 14 years. So, how did it all come about? Back in the mid-1990s I was a life coach coaching clients to have more success in their work. Some of my clients were concerned about where their time was going. They told me they would get to work, start work on a couple of projects and suddenly it was lunchtime. Before they knew it the day was over. Where had all their time gone and why had they accomplished so little? To find out, I asked them to track their time on paper every 30 minutes of the working day. We discovered that time, apart from the unavoidable amount spent traveling, was disappearing into two main areas: meetings and reading. For the first area, I gathered information on running a tidy meeting, with tools like deciding in advance how long to give each topic, assigning a time keeper and ending the meeting at the time that was agreed upon, no matter what.

Then there was reading. What could be done? One option we considered was to hire someone else to read material and provide an executive brief highlighting the main points. The problem was that important items could be missed or misinterpreted. Another option was to transcribe written work to audiotape, but focusing on what is being said can be difficult, going back over bits you've missed is cumbersome and it can take even longer than reading. Or, of course, they could just ignore the material. Unfortunately, that could have serious consequences. As one client, a manager at Sun Microsystems, said: "Fifteen years ago I could just go to trade shows and keep up to date on the industry. Ten years ago I could read quarterly synopses of what was happening and not fall behind. Five years ago I could just about get away with monthly newsletters. Now that the industry has become so competitive and fast-paced, and I'm a high-level manager making multi-million-dollar decisions, I need information almost daily because things can change so quickly. I must be totally up to date or we could lose millions. And I can't trust anyone else to know what I need. That's why I took this course."

I looked into "speed reading" to see if that would help. It was sort of OK for novels, but for business or legal reading it just didn't help people to get everything they needed and not miss important points. So I experimented. I got people together and tried various techniques. The techniques that were successful went on to form the backbone of the SuperReading™ course. While SuperReading™ is related to speed reading, this book focuses on comprehension first. I feel that going fast is meaningless if you do not understand what you've read and cannot recall it. Traditional "speed reading" courses get you to skip words and sometimes whole sections of what you are reading. With SuperReading™ you do not have to do that. You will read every word and understand it while going faster and faster over time.

The most important development I devised was the Eye-Hop™ exercises (see chapter 8). I had heard that it was important to read in groups of words, instead of just one word at a time. So I worked at a series of exercises with words separated into groups and found that regular practice reading these allowed people to surpass their present speeds greatly, while maintaining or even improving their comprehension. The Eye-Hop™ exercises are the hallmark of SuperReading™ and you will find examples on pages 126–31.

Who could this book help?

This book could benefit anyone who is reading at the level of a nine-year-old or better. Since 1996 the Super-Reading™ course has been taken by engineers, doctors, lawyers, dentists, managers, university students, students at all levels, salespeople, administrative assistants, teachers, professors, researchers, moms, dads and grandparents. It has been taken by fast readers, slow readers, pleasure readers, business readers, dyslexics, children and adults with attention deficit hyperactivity disorder (ADHD), avid readers and people who (previously) hated reading. The basics of SuperReading™ are appropriate for people of any age, but some of the high-level Eye-Hop™ exercises (see chapter 8 for all you need to know about this) may be too sophisticated for most primary school children, depending on their mental development.

What will you gain from this book?

Once you have worked your way through this book you will have learned some simple skills and techniques which will improve your ability to focus, read, retain and recall information. You will know when you are taking in what you have read and when you are not. You will be able to regain and maintain your concentration when it slips. You will become confident that whatever the reading challenge you are presented with, you have the best tools for doing a great job with it. You will feel assured that even when your reading stack is high you will be able to get through it in record time. You will also find you can get past dry, poorly written material and glean just what you need from it. Your self-esteem will rise as you realize you can perform brilliantly.

Remember: whenever students, of any age, apply these simple techniques, they tend to rise to the top of their class. Here is a comment from a professional in Silicon Valley, California:

CASE STUDY

Hi Ron,

I took your SuperReading™ class earlier this year, along with my co-worker, Tim. As you know, we are both taking an MBA program that involves night classes. For the last year, we have been going each week, and seeing our standing in the course among our 100+ peers.

Our professor posts the grades outside the door each week. We see our student number, our grade, and our ranking in the class. In the past, before your class, our ranking was all over the grid. One week I could be number 7, the next week 101 and the following week number 75. Since the third week of SuperReading™, Tim and I have occupied the number 1 and 2 positions, and nobody can surpass us! Each week we jockey between ourselves and the rest of the class has to fight for number 3.

To us, this demonstrates the power of the skills we learned from you. In a way, we're no smarter than we were before SuperReading™. What we have is the ability to understand and recall what we read. Perhaps we are smarter. It depends on how one defines intelligence. Either way, our reading skills have set us above about 120 other professionals struggling to enhance their careers.

So we both send you a big "thank you." We're spending half the time studying and getting far better results. It's just how you said it would be.

FRANK T., ENGINEER, ADVANCED MICRO DEVICES (AMD)

Frank's comment neatly sums up the benefits of Super-Reading™. Frank and Tim cut out half the time they spent studying and were the best in their class. All it took was about three weeks' study with good tools. The "full effect" of SuperReading™ means *all* the tools coming together, making them as brilliant a reader as they will become while they are on the course. With Frank, as with most people, he did not require the "full effect" to rise to the top of the class, and achieved high levels within three weeks. Because many people's reading and recalling skills are so poor, they do not require the full effect of SuperReading™ to overtake others. Frank and Tim completed the course in about the year 2000. This book in your hands now has even better tools than Frank and Tim had available to them. Apply them and you too will be the best reader in your group. However, if everyone in your group has bought this book, then all bets are off! What's really important is that you become the best reader you can be.

"Your biggest competitor is your own view of your future."

WATTS WACKER AND JIM TAYLOR

(lecturers and business people, authors of *The 500-Year Delta*)

How long will it take before I see some results?

SuperReading™ is not a pill you take or a jab in the arm to make you a better reader. It's a series of simple concepts combined together to make a powerful set of tools. Most people who take the course will see significant improvement in their comprehension within a few days. They notice that they drift off less and retain information better. Some see a qualitative difference in the first hour or two. For the full effect of all the tools to come together takes most people five to seven weeks. Some people have accomplished this in as little as three weeks, but that is quite rare.

As the memory tools come into play retention is increased. After the first two months you can experience a slow and steady gain from that point. For example, you may begin the course with a Reading Effectiveness (R.E.) score of 100 (for a full explanation of R.E. scores, see page 309). Three weeks later it may be in the 300 range. After six or seven weeks it may be in the 500 to 800 range. After ten weeks you could reach 1,000 to 1,500. After that, if you keep practicing the advanced techniques and the growth techniques, it is possible to surpass 2,000 within another three months, around twenty weeks in total. While few people achieve this, it is only because of other commitments and the fact that they are very happy with R.E. scores of around 600 to 800, which already makes reading much more fun, efficient and worthwhile.

SuperReading™ skills will save you around 20,000 hours in a typical career. Some people will save more time than that. Whether you are reading for pleasure, study, work, self-development or any other reason, these skills will bring both efficiency and pleasure to your efforts.

The key to success

The key to success in SuperReading™ is to follow the steps like you would a recipe for a cake. Reading the lessons doesn't take very long at all. Even with your present reading skills you could read all the lessons in an hour or two. It's not so much a question of knowing what's in this book; it's more about practicing it. Most of the tools in the book you can simply read about and begin using straight away. However, the Eye-Hop™ exercises (you will find out about these in chapter 8) require 40 minutes of investment per day and will take between four and eight weeks to master. Once you've mastered them, the benefits will last you the rest of your life.

"Striving for success without hard work is like trying to harvest where you haven't planted."

DAVID BLY
(politician and writer)

What if I don't like reading?

Some people in my courses hated reading. It seemed like hard work to them. They were looking to change that because their job required them to read volumes. Like them, probably the reason you don't like reading is that it has been difficult for you. It feels like work because, for you, it is work! I have observed people go from hating reading to loving it after doing the SuperReading™ course. This is especially true for young people, though age is only a consideration if you allow it to be. The bottom line is that when you can do something really well with relatively little effort, you don't mind it so much. If you need to read, or at least understand how vital it can be to your success, your new skills can motivate you to do more and improve.

Now it all comes down to attitude. If you are open and willing to give it an honest go, you will see that reading can be fairly effortless and quite rewarding. Just hang in there and keep at it for a while. If you have a positive attitude it will open you up to more possibilities. Your brain will respond and give you a more positive experience.

"Your Attitude determines your Aptitude which determines your Altitude!"

BOB MOAWAD
(motivational speaker)

How will I know I'm progressing?

You may be wondering about what benchmarks or signs will be good indicators of your progress. You already know the time frames of what to expect in terms of days, weeks and months. I realize we're living in a society that often expects instant gratification and results. Many of the skills in this book can work "straight out of the box." However, it depends on how you are doing at any particular moment. A tool that might get great results for you on Thursday may not have had the same effect on Tuesday. That is why it's so important to reserve judgment (I talk more about this in chapter 4). ALL of the tools in this book CAN work; the real questions will be which ones work best for you or which way they will work best for you.

CASE STUDY

The early groups I taught, back in the mid-1990s, were only tested on their reading speed on the first day of the course. Four weeks after her reading test one woman commented that she felt her speed hadn't increased much at all. Her reading speed felt the same to her, although she thought her comprehension was definitely greater. I gave her group another speed test at four weeks. Her speed had risen from 175 w.p.m. to 660 w.p.m. She was astounded. This happens because each day we "normalize" to our new speed. She ended up reading novels from a speed of 800 w.p.m. to well over 1,000 w.p.m.

When we grow gradually we often cannot see the changes happening. If you've ever had the experience of not seeing a child for a year or two, and then you see them again, they look far bigger to you. To their parents the changes are less noticeable because they are with them every day. You may find the same experience with your reading. During classes I get reports from my students. They sometimes say how a colleague has commented on how quickly they are reading. Sometimes this takes them by surprise, as they have not noticed the change in their reading themselves.

This book comes with a set of tests that will help you to gauge your own progress in both speed and recall. The tests are quite rigorous and in different subjects, and will represent a fairly accurate estimate of your abilities. There is also another method, personal testing, which will test you on areas you already have an interest in (see page 68). You may find these results will be more rewarding and accurate. Mostly your scores will go up from week to week. Occasionally they go down, but don't worry; this is normal and may be due to a number of factors from sleep to stress to your interest in the subject, and whether you have recently begun a new reading skill. With all that in mind, you will be amazed how your scores do generally go up over time, despite all the factors that can affect reading.

The testing section will help you determine your present reading abilities. These tests are important; they will help you measure your progress. While skipping them would get you into the lessons more quickly, the lessons are only an hour away! I strongly recommend doing the testing.

What else is in this book?

This book will not only cover powerful reading skills, but also the power of attitude, affirmation, learning and memory. Let's start with attitude!

"Whether you think you can do a thing, or whether you think you can't, you're probably right!"

HENRY FORD
(Founder of Ford Motor Company)

Your brain believes what you tell it. If you are convinced that you can do something, you are virtually unstoppable. If you are convinced that you will fail at something, your brain will find many creative ways *not to* succeed (in other words, fail). Think of this book as being like a recipe. Follow the instructions and the "cake" will taste great. Leave out any of the ingredients and it will not come out as you hoped. Here's my most important thought on that: given enough time and effort, you can become a super reader, absorbing information quickly, accurately, and recalling it when you need to. The ONLY question is how long it will take you, not IF you can.

The other components of the book revolve around useful skills and tools such as developing your vocabulary, spellings, Info-Mapping™, note taking, visualizing and setting goals. The more of these you employ, the sooner your reading and recall skills will grow to full potential. You may or may not see all the relationships between and among these various skill sets. Each one can help build others. For example, taking notes after you read will demonstrate to you how much more you are recalling. That feedback can enhance your attitude, which may help you accept some of the more esoteric concepts, such as visualization and affirmation (see chapter 12). Success with those may spur you to try developing another area you may not have otherwise considered. The more positive steps you take, the better the results.

Why are SuperReading™ skills so important today?

In order to cope with today's reading demands you can't be using 19th-century skills. E-mail alone threatens to overwhelm many people. Unless you are immortal, you must budget your time. Why spend three hours reading a document when you could do a better job of it in one hour? Most of us have so much to do. We have projects on hold and more waiting in the wings after those. By investing a few hours following the techniques explained in this book you can save hundreds of hours per year. The average U.S.

employee now spends an average of 15½ hours per week reading. That's up from 7½ hours per week in 1996. You can reclaim those lost hours with the skills you learn from this book. The next six weeks of your life will go by in a flash whether you do this or not. Imagine—had you started this a mere six weeks ago, today you would have read this far in less than half the time and actually remembered most of it!

"The illiterate of the 21st century will not be those who cannot read and write, but those who cannot learn, unlearn and relearn."

ALVIN TOFFLER
(writer and futurist)

A part of you may well be wondering if you can really double your reading abilities. That may not seem possible. In fact, it's not only possible, it's inevitable. Once you understand how you will measure your progress it becomes clearer. Let's start with reading speed. Most people read around 150 to 200 words per minute (w.p.m.). Easy novels could be read from 200 to 300 w.p.m. or a bit faster (though with lower comprehension). Difficult textbooks could be 100 w.p.m. or slower. Taking 200 w.p.m. as an average, if you ended up reading similar material at 400 w.p.m., you would have doubled your speed. If you look at the speed charts in Appendix D, this will become clear.

Moving on to consider average comprehension/recall, this is between 30 and 60 percent at comfortable speeds (200 w.p.m.). Average comprehension/recall above 320 w.p.m. will probably be quite low, around 20 to 40 percent. When you boost that to 80 percent comprehension after following the advice in this book, you've more than doubled your effectiveness again. Combining both figures means you've quadrupled it.

In short, this book will teach you the skills you need to absorb information in today's ever changing world of learning. Information content will change over time, but our brains and the basic way they function will not. Prepare to learn how to take better advantage of that wonderful brain of yours. No matter what you may have thought of it in the past, it has only performmed to the level at which it was taught and programmed. You are about to take it to the next level with the right tools and a little encouragement. So listen well: YOU CAN DO THIS! You have been duly encouraged!

"There comes a moment when you realize that virtually anything is possible—that nothing is too good to be true."

KOBI YAMADA

(CEO of Compendium Inc., a leading strategic communications company)

SUMMARY

- Anyone can greatly increase their reading abilities in just a few weeks, by following the advice in this book.

- You will have to put in some effort to achieving these improvements, but probably less than you think.

- If you have the right attitude you will do even better.

- Improved reading skills will allow you to read and understand more in less time, reducing stress and allowing you to recall more information.

- As Benjamin Franklin said, "Time is money."

2.

Overcoming your reading challenges

want you to become a confident, excellent reader. This means that you are able to approach a reading "assignment" intelligently and enthusiastically, getting all you need from it in a relatively short amount of time. Also, you will have the tools and ability to retain whatever you wish, for as long as you wish. And I want you to continue to use your improved skills so they will continue to improve. I want you to read anything and get the most you can from it in the least amount of time, and enjoy the process.

I do realize that you may have specific concerns or worries about your ability to benefit from this book. Before I go on to address some of these worries, I can honestly say that in 14 years of teaching people Super-Reading™ only one person on one of my courses has not been helped; a woman whose eye muscles had been badly damaged in a car crash and was unable to move her eyes without moving her head. So, unless you have similar serious eyesight issues, you will be able to benefit from this course. Indeed, you will be able to do brilliantly.

I can't anticipate all your concerns in this chapter, but here are some questions I am often asked by students before they take the course.

What if my eyesight is not all it should be?

 Reading is a visual art. If you can't see, you can't read. If you need corrective eyewear you should take care of this before starting the course. If your eyesight is a problem, you may not reap all the benefits you are other-wise capable of achieving. If you have any doubts at all about your eyesight, you should consider visiting a "behavioral optometrist." These are vision specialists who look for problems that may not be picked up by conventional optometrists. They offer training classes that can solve problems such as:

- eyes tracking too far inward or outward
- eyes not focusing where you're looking
- sensitivity to certain wavelengths of light
- severe eye dominance (where the brain accepts only limited amounts of information from one eye in favor of the dominant eye).

Each of these problems can be "fixed" with relative ease. There are other problems they can help with, which are more technical. These thorough eye exams can be especially important for children.

What if I read really slowly?

You may be wondering if this course can help you even if you're a really slow reader. The answer is yes it can and yes it will, as the following example shows:

CASE STUDY

A mother called me to ask about her daughter who was the slowest reader in her school. When all the other children had finished a reading assignment she was barely halfway through. To make it worse she had poor recall of the text. A friend whose son had been through the course was doing really well. The mother, a doctor, was about to have her daughter tested to check for learning disabilities and other possible problems. Before putting her through that the friend convinced her to give Super-Reading™ a try. Luckily I was running a course that very weekend. Two weeks later this young girl was the fastest and best reader in her class, and three weeks later was the best in her school. After the course there was no question that she was the best and also no question that there was anything wrong with her. All she needed were some good tools, which did wonders for her self-image, and she later improved in all subjects.

Being a slow reader is usually just a sign of poor reading tools. In the following chapters you will be learning simple tools that will have a profound impact on your reading. By adopting these tools and techniques you will speed up and get more out of your reading.

What if I'm a bit of a perfectionist?

Are you afraid you'll miss something if you go fast? While that is a legitimate concern, you need not worry. You will always be in control of your speed. You will NOT be like a car with the accelerator pedal stuck down. While there is virtue in being careful in order to get it right, soon your brain will be working faster by natural means. What will feel slow to you will be quite a bit faster than you read today. The difference is the skills you will develop between now and then. Remember the lady in chapter 1 who thought she wasn't reading any faster? She may have been just as careful as before. The fact is that you will be reading in a more focused and concentrated way. As your competence increases, you will be able to handle more material in less time while paying attention to detail. The difference is that you won't have to get stressed over it.

It's a good idea to let go of the concept of perfection. It is not attainable. It is a myth; a dangerous, frustrating and sometimes debilitating myth. Replace it with the concept of excellence, which can actually be achieved.

The key is in knowing when to stop. Once you've achieved excellence, walk away; you're finished. Besides, you know that all that extra effort you put into things isn't always appreciated by most people anyway. Only you know the difference.

> **ASSIGNMENT**
>
> For the next 21 days, be aware of when you have achieved excellence with projects you undertake. Once you get there, say to yourself, "I have achieved enough with this. I'm going to let it go now and watch the consequences." Track your projects and see what happens.

What if I tend to drift off when reading?

Do you drift off a lot while you are reading? Do you keep losing the plot and sometimes have to reread entire sections? Help is on the way. There are two tools that you will get in the first couple of lessons in the book—pointing and previewing (see pages 75 and 92)—that will virtually eliminate that phenomenon, which I call "distracted reader syndrome." One of the causes of this syndrome is reading too slowly. Your brain believes it can multitask and think about other things. It has learned how to fool you into thinking you are reading by pronouncing the words in your head but not processing them deeply. This book will help you become more aware and keep your focus.

What if I am already a fast reader?

What if you believe you are already a fast reader? What can this book do for you? In fact, fast readers are often poor recallers. I've had loads of people join a course because the company needed more delegates to justify the cost. Some people came in believing they were already superior readers. What they found was that they had high speed, but low comprehension and recall. They would argue that for their job all they needed to do was scan material for a few important points and they had become very good at that. Others felt they were "very fast readers" and didn't really need to learn anything more, but they felt it might be handy to pick up a pointer or two.

What they realized was that they had probably missed some important points over the years by skimming instead of reading. They were able to achieve even higher speeds while increasing their comprehension and recall. They were previously unaware that their recall had been so low.

What if I have dyslexia or other learning challenges?

I've had many people in my classes with dyslexia, dyspraxia and other barriers to reading/learning. I have seen them all make significant progress in their reading and recalling abilities. While some of them have not achieved as highly as non-dyslexic delegates overall, two things were fairly consistent. One was that their "ratio of improvement" was on par with non-challenged learners. That is to say, if most people saw a five-fold increase in their overall abilities from their starting point, so did people with learning challenges. The other interesting factor is that most of the dyslexic learners ended up with higher numerical scores than non-challenged readers without SuperReading™ skills.

In a 2008 study of adult dyslexic students at London South Bank University, they all saw significant improvement as a result of taking the SuperReading™ course. One of the surprising findings was that those coming in with the poorest abilities saw some of the largest gains.

Here is an interesting quote from Dr. Ross Cooper, principal lecturer, London Southbank University: "When we piloted SuperReading™ with a group of dyslexic students at London Southbank University, their reading effectiveness more than doubled in ten weeks. I have known nothing like it. I have always advocated individual support for dyslexic students, but this impact was achieved in a group of 15. Just imagine how much better their university learning experience would have been had they completed the course before starting their studies."

How SuperReading™ overcomes the problems of "standard reading"

The way we were taught to read at school (known as "standard reading") is adequate, but it is not effective enough for today's informational demands. Whether people are taught "phonics" or "real reading," the methods of reading that are taught in most schools as a standard have inherent problems concerning concentration, comprehension and retention. The so-called information superhighway implies high speed and high volume; but we are limited by our ability to absorb the information we need in the time we have available. The following pitfalls hold us back. My feeling is that knowing and understanding these pitfalls will aid you in overcoming them.

"He who has a why can endure any how."

FRIEDRICH NIETZSCHE

1. Unconscious and conscious regression

Regression means "to go back." Both conscious and unconscious regression cause problems for readers, but the techniques of SuperReading™ can deal with both effectively.

Unconscious regression

We may believe that our eyes track straight across the page when we read, but special sensors reveal that the eyes can wander as much as 18 times per minute. This is known as unconscious regression and is a source of poor concentration, since we are "reading" in one place while our eyes look in another place. You will learn two tools (pointing and previewing in chapters 6 and 7) that will help you overcome this regression.

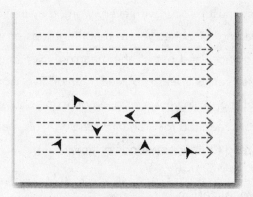

Unconscious regression

Conscious regression

Another form of regression occurs when we stop, back up and read something we have just read (or tried to read). While this makes some sense for a standard reader, it really holds us back from having higher comprehension. The same two tools of pointing and previewing referred to above will help with this form of regression as well.

The quick brown fox jumps over the lazy dog.

2. Reading word by word

While reading one word at a time was necessary in our earliest days at school, nobody ever told us how to progress on to reading multiple words at a time. One problem with reading word by word is that our eyes get tired! The eye muscles are among the weakest in the human body and when they must refocus with every word, they begin to tire. SuperReading™ teaches you to read in groups of words at a single glance—and get all the meaning! (See chapter 8.) Over time, you will learn to read four or five words at a glance (or more), so your eyes need only do about one-fifth of the work required for standard reading. This means that you can read for longer periods of time.

3. Sub-vocalization

Pronouncing the words we are reading in our head is known as sub-vocalization. This is a limitation because we cannot read and comprehend well much faster than we can speak, and top speech speed for most humans is about 300 w.p.m. By reading four or five words at a glance using SuperReading™ techniques, the brain gives up on trying to "say" the words, and simply understands the meaning without pronouncing them all. When you are able to read several words at once, you will notice that as your speed goes up, so too does your comprehension. This would seem to defy logic, but only with your present reading tools. When you can see and understand a group of words at a time, you are able to engage more of your "right brain," which is capable of tremendous understanding.

In the 1960s experiments showed that the two sides of the human brain were responsible for different functions. It was discovered that information from your left eye goes to your right brain, and information from your right eye goes to your left brain, with the optic nerves crossing one another behind your forehead. It seems that your left brain is mostly verbal, logical, numerical and serial, while your right brain is pictorial, spatial, holistic, creative, nonlinear, musical, arty, intuitive and emotional. Most people tend toward one or the other. The ideal is to have balance or synergy between the two. People who combine right-brain inspiration with left-brain logic often transcend ordinary accomplishments. Celebrated examples would be Leonardo da Vinci, Einstein and Michelangelo. By using their whole brain, they were able to think in ways other people found difficult or impossible. When you read using more of your right brain you have a fuller experience of the text. Stories come alive when you are able to see and experience a book. Business reading can improve as well. Indeed, any experience where you can involve both sides of the brain will be positively enhanced.

4. Poor vocabulary

> ARE YOU FAMILIAR WITH THE WORDS
> IN BOLD?
>
> **Sargute** – shrewd
>
> **Ascesis** – self-discipline
>
> **Cromulent** – acceptable
>
> **Freck** – to move quickly
>
> **Halcyon** – calm
>
> **Redolent** – fragrant

If you don't understand enough of the words you read, your comprehension will suffer. SuperReading™ has a system to help you record, understand and recall new words. (See pages 241–2.) Vocabulary is an important area of life. People judge us by the words we use. Your ability to think is either helped or hampered by your vocabulary. If you don't know a word you cannot think of that concept in order to solve a problem or express a point. Building up a resource of useful words will help you become a better reader (and writer as well).

5. Poor organization
Most people simply pick up a book and start reading. When they reach the end they put it down and move on to something else. They employ no effective strategies for extracting the information they need and remembering anything that is vital. SuperReading™ teaches

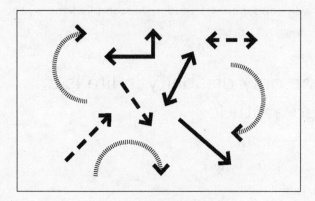

Poor organization

you strategies to improve your organization, including a few minutes of eye exercises each day.

6. Poor attitude

Many people believe themselves to be poor readers and worry that there's little that can be done to fix their situation. They may even tell themselves and others what a slow reader they are. Some people become cynical, and do not believe that new tools can help them. These people can be their own worst enemy. They may have tried some things before and found them to be less helpful than expected. Usually, they have not reserved judgment (see pages 44–7) and thereby not given those tools adequate practice.

Please note: I've taught thousands of people and can confirm that those who doubt either themselves or the tools end up performing the most poorly. Negative attitudes yield negative results. People who expect to do well (and persist) tend to accomplish more, and in less time.

"The only disability in life is a bad attitude."

SCOTT HAMILTON
(Olympic ice skater)

Another important point is that for many people, their greatest progress comes toward the end of the course. Once again, please reserve judgment on your skills and on your progress until the end of the book.

"The key to everything is patience. You get the chicken by hatching the egg, not by smashing it."

ARNOLD H. GLASOW
(frequently quoted humor writer)

SUMMARY

- You will have a few challenges to overcome before you can become a super reader, potentially ranging from problems with your eyesight to a poor attitude, but follow the advice in this book and you will succeed.

- The only thing you don't know exactly is how many weeks it will take you (but note, I am not saying months or years).

- Using the tools in this book will help you overcome just about any challenge you will face in your quest to be a super reader. Just stay with it, be patient and you will succeed.

3.

Before you begin

I believe it's important to understand how you learn things. With that knowledge you can look out for learning opportunities that play to your strengths. You can also put some effort into bolstering the areas in which you are weak. This is useful because often it's not possible to control how information is presented to us. We must take it as it comes.

There are many different types of learners, and there are two main ways to determine the type of learner you are: the psychological and the physical. Let's look at the psychological first.

The psychology of learning

There is a spectrum of attitudes among learners, ranging from people who are not interested in learning at all to people who are very eager to learn, understand the benefits and put in every effort to master a new skill regardless of any obstacles. They jump in with both feet and are certain that they will conquer this new thing. Most people fall somewhere in between the two extremes. Near the top are people who understand and appreciate the benefits of SuperReading™ and are looking forward to giving it a go. Near the bottom are people who are very skeptical and are tempted to abandon ship at the first setback or when they realize it might take a lot of time or effort. In between are those who are skeptical but rather hopeful. It goes without saying that the people at the lower end of the spectrum make life much harder for themselves. Their cynical views hamper their ability to learn (see the brain scan experiment on page 221).

Where do you fit on the psychology of learning scale?

1 Not interested in learning (prisoner to your past experience/beliefs)

2 Very skeptical, but will take a small chance

3 Skeptical, but hopeful

4 Fairly confident, need to experience it

5 Fairly committed, only vague doubts

6 Appreciate benefits, will give it a go

7 Very eager, will master new skills no matter what (take no prisoners).

It is really important to work out where you are on the psychology of learning scale. If your attitude isn't right, the rest hardly matters. As you will soon learn, your brain will work to the capability in which you believe in yourself. The skills in this book are not rocket science. While innovative, they are really quite simple. As simple as they are, a cleverly cynical brain can usually find a way to sabotage just about anything. Only your attitude that this can work (by putting in enough good effort) can save you from the fate of the truly cynical. Their fate is to miss out on the best skills and abilities because they did not give themselves a fair chance to embody them.

Visual, audio and kinesthetic (VAK) learning

When it comes to the physical aspects of learning people are divided into visual, audio and kinesthetic learners. Visual people learn mainly through their eyes. The world makes sense to them when they can **see** the meaning or how something works. Audio (or aural) people **hear** how things work. There are two kinds of audio learners: analog and digital. Analog audio people learn by hearing sounds from outside their body. Digital audio people learn by repeating what they hear outside internally using their "inner voice." Kinesthetic people must **touch or experience** something in order to learn it well. They learn best by doing. They can also experience the emotional aspects of what they are learning.

The representational system preference test

This brief quiz (also known as the Rep Test) will give you an indication of how your brain likes to process information from your environment. There will be more explanation after you answer the five questions. Please read the instructions very carefully.

For each of the following statements, please place a number next to every phrase. Use the following system to indicate your preferences:

> 4................*Closest to describing you*
>
> 3................*Next best description*
>
> 2................*Next best*
>
> 1................*Least descriptive of you*

Use all four numbers in each of the five sections—there are NO ties in a section.

1.   I make important decisions based on:

................gut-level feelings

................which way sounds best

................what looks best to me

................precise review and study of the issues

2.   During an argument, I am most likely to be influenced by:

................the other person's tone of voice

................whether or not I can see the other person's argument

..................the logic of the other person's argument

..................whether or not I feel I am in touch with the other person's true feelings

3.   **I most easily communicate what is going on with me by:**

..................the way I dress and look

..................the feelings I share

..................the words I choose

..................the tone of my voice

4.   **It is easier for me to:**

..................find the ideal volume and tuning on a stereo system

..................select the most intellectually relevant point concerning an interesting subject

..................select the most comfortable furniture

..................select rich, attractive color combinations

5. ....I am very attuned to the sounds of my environment

..................I am very adept at making sense of new facts and data

..................I am very sensitive to the way articles of clothing feel on my body

..................I have a strong response to colors and to the way a room looks

Now bring down your values and write them in for each question:

1: _____   **2:** _____   **3:** _____   **4:** _____   **5:** _____

K _____   A _____   V _____   A _____   A _____

A _____   V _____   K _____   D _____   D _____

V _____   D _____   D _____   K _____   K _____

D _____   K _____   A _____   V _____   V _____

Now add up the values for each letter (add all the "Vs" together, then all the "Ks," etc.)

V............................ Visual   K............................ Kinesthetic

A............................ Analog Audio   D............................ Digital Audio

Interpreting the Rep Test

The questions in the Rep Test were designed to discover what kinds of information your brain prefers to use to understand the world. For example, how do you get your news each day? You have choices of newspapers, TV, radio, friends, the internet, cable and satellite broadcasts. Which do you prefer? If that was not available, what would your second choice be? And your third choice? Any of those choices will tell you what's happening, but you will prefer one choice over another. The Rep Test will tell you which sensory modality you tend to prefer. Now, read on to see what your scores tell you about how you like to learn. The first three answers tell you about your intuitive nature and the last two tell you about your physical relationship to the environment.

V stands for Visual. This is information that comes in through your eyes.

K stands for Kinesthetic. This involves a combination of emotional feelings and body awareness.

A stands for Analog Audio. Take your fingers and make a tapping sound on your table or desk. That tapping caused the molecules in the table to vibrate. They in turn caused the air molecules to vibrate. That reached your inner ear and caused your eardrum to vibrate. Those vibrations became nerve impulses and reached your brain. At that moment you experienced the sound. "A" stands for the sounds that are outside of you in the environment.

D stands for Digital Audio. Right now, sing to yourself the words to "Happy Birthday." Did you hear it in your head? Yes? That is Digital Audio. You experienced hearing, but the "sound" did not originate in the outside environment (with vibrating air molecules). It started and ended inside your head. That is very different from Analog Audio, which is a more passive experience.

What the scores indicate:
Anything **12 and above** is significant.
Anything **16 and above** is highly significant.
Anything **19 and above** is rare. With these scores you

are so dominated by that mode that special allowances should be made. You have so much dependence in that area of input that it can be seen as both a real advantage when available and a possible handicap when denied. For example, a person who has a very high Visual score and a very low Analog Audio score will have a difficult time learning in a classroom where lecture is the only delivery method.

A score of 7 or below is relatively rare. It would almost seem that the brain is avoiding that mode for some reason. Remember, there is a default of 5 even if a mode scores last in all 5 categories!

Over time your scores can change. You can train yourself in any area and your brain will respond by giving that mode a chance. This is especially true of Visual and Kinesthetic learning. You can train your Visual mode by using the picture visualization technique (see page 192).

Most important, remember that this test indicates your preference. Even a score of 10 or less does not necessarily mean you are not good at that skill. It simply means that skill or modality is not your brain's first choice when it goes about interpreting the world. It's only a rule of thumb. Do NOT get carried away with this test. Always see your outcomes as advantages.

ASSIGNMENT

Taking into consideration what you have learned about how you learn, make one change per day about how you take in information, either in reading, listening or observing. For example, if you are a kinesthetic learner, a hands-on course would be better for you than a lecture only. You learn primarily by doing, touching and trying. If you are primarily an analog audio person, a lecture is fine, as you can easily interpret words and do not need to experience a concept to understand it.

SUMMARY

- Knowing what kind of learner you are is an advantage to a super reader; you can learn to play to your strengths.

- If you are a visual learner, sit at the front of the class or lecture theater. Whatever the teacher puts on the board will be inspiring and stimulating to you.

- If you are more of an analog audio learner, you can sit further back, as long as you can hear what the teacher is saying.

- If you are a kinesthetic learner, try to find courses that supply hands-on experience. You will learn better by touching, doing and manipulating objects.

- If you are digital audio, you need to be able to repeat things to yourself verbally. You could also verbally explain the material to someone else. You work best when you can hear your voice in your head.

4.

Reserving judgment and setting goals

The purpose of this chapter is to instill in you an open mind and a willingness to stretch beyond your present understandings and limitations. That is what the concept of reserving judgment is all about and why it is so important to SuperReading™ success. Once you have come to grips with reserving judgment it's time to set yourself some goals and really put your newfound commitment into practice. The concept of ideation or brainstorming is also useful for generating ideas and stretching yourself.

Reserving judgment

 Imagine you are going on a voyage across the sea. You leave port and set sail for a distant land. You're out there on the vast, open waters. You're making good time, but it's a big ocean! There are days and days of nothing but sea and sky. Finally, you spot land and make port soon after. Dry land at last! Thinking back, you realise that

for 99 percent of your voyage you could not see your destination! You had charts and a compass, but until you actually saw the land, and the desired port, there was no other real proof that things were going well.

Achieving something can be much the same as that sea voyage. Very often we can't see any perceptible change or progress until we're near the end, and then suddenly it's there. We realize that we have achieved what we set out to do. Faith and persistence have helped many people achieve seemingly impossible tasks.

Learning a new skill can also be compared to a sea voyage. Or consider a ten-month-old child learning to walk. They have bumbled around for weeks or months barely able to stand. They wobble and fall many times. Then, one day, suddenly, they're walking! Before they know it they're running! A child learning to walk is the perfect example of faith and persistence in action, and it will be helpful to remember this mindset as you go through the book.

New skills take time, and even when you master a skill it may be that you do not see its apparent benefit right away. You have to keep on going long enough to give it a fair chance to work for you. This is where the concept of reserving judgment really comes into play. If you're feeling that a new skill is not paying off, you're being prematurely judgmental and not giving it adequate time to work for you.

There is no substitute for experience. Intellectually understanding something is not the same as doing the thing. You will receive the most benefit from this book if you reserve your judgment and keep practicing the skills. Although you can be taking tests each week, the time for measuring your full progress is after you have absorbed and mastered all the skills. Arguing with the ideas presented here will not help you. Indeed, some of these ideas may defy your traditional sense of logic. However, if you learn these ideas and push ahead with them, they will benefit you for the rest of your life. Only by practice, persistence and finally mastery will these skills have a lasting, positive impact on your life. So relax and enjoy the voyage.

Contract with yourself

Before you go any further, take a look at the following contract, which defines what is meant by reserving judgment, and if you want to go further, sign it now!

I understand the significance of practicing a specific new skill for at least 21 days (or 21 times) before I decide whether it is valuable to me.

I declare my willingness and determination to fully apply each new skill that I learn.

I declare that I will practice each new skill with enthusiasm and diligence for at least 21 days in a row, and then and only then consider its effectiveness.

SIGNATURE..

DATE...

ASSIGNMENT

After you have signed your contract with yourself, for the next 21 days carry a card with you that says, "I am reserving judgment." Look at it at least five times per day and jot down notes about the times you have found it helpful. After the 21 days are up, write down your thoughts about the assignment you have just carried out. In what areas of your life did reserving judgment make a difference? You may be surprised how effective it is and how often it can come into play.

Setting goals

 It is very important to have goals, both in life and, more specifically for the purposes of this book, in your reading. Those people who regularly set clear goals and keep after them tend to achieve them. In my work as a personal coach, the first thing I do is get people to write down what it is that they want to achieve. I suggest you do the same.

The categories listed below are suggestions for the kinds of things you can look forward to reading. Simply write down a list of all the things you would like to either become an expert in or would just like to know more about. Whenever you hear about a book or subject that intrigues you set it down as a goal to preview (for more on this see page 99) or read.

You can put a time frame to it if you like. You may want

to put down those things you would like to read in the next six months, in the next two years and the next five years. If you like, you can also prioritize your reading, not just by dates but by letters. Give a rating of "A" to the books that are of most importance in your life now. Give a "B" to those that are significant but not critical. Give a "C" to those that you'll get to some day. You can put both a deadline for completing a book and one for starting the book. Sometimes the start dates hold more power than the end dates! Keep referring back to your list at least once a week. Every day is even better if you can manage it.

When you have read them, take notes on these materials using the note-taking method explained on pages 147–51. You can keep a separate notebook for all the things you have learned. It feels good when you can check off a book you had written down for reading. As the months go by you will be surprised at how many books you will have read using these methods. And with Super-Reading™, you will have really read them!

When goal setting, the rule is:

Be brave,
Be bold,
Believe.

Then be relentless.

Reading goals

Write down goals for what you would like to read in the months and years ahead. Draw up a list of books, magazines, journals and authors you are particularly interested in. You could make an Info-Map™ (see chapter 10) of your ideas and add to it as you come across more reading materials that you would like to read. With each, write down a start date and a completion date. Check them off as you complete them!

Here are some headings to get you started:

- Autobiographies
- Biographies
- How-to
- Inspirational
- Self-development
- Spiritual

And don't forget to include subjects relating to your own particular hobbies and interests.

> "You must have long-range goals to keep you from being frustrated by short-range failures."

CHARLES C. NOBLE

(former Dean of Syracuse University, 1946)

ASSIGNMENT

Review your goals in the first 30 minutes of your day and in the last 30 minutes of your day. That's all you need to do. Actions will follow automatically.

Ideation

Ideation (formerly known as brainstorming) has been around for a long time and is a useful tool to help you generate ideas. Start with a blank sheet of paper. Visualize it full of great ideas, and then begin to write. Extend two lines out from every idea (whether you use the idea or not). Do not judge whether a thought is good or not. Just write it down. To get to buried treasure, you must dig through loads of dirt. Most of what you come up with will be fairly useless, but that's OK and is expected. As two-time Nobel Prize winner Linus Pauling said, "To have a great idea you must have many ideas."

You can fill several pages this way. If you feel you've run out of ideas, visualize more, then put pen to paper and start it moving again. More ideas will come to you. When your first piece of ideation is finally complete, circle the best ideas. You can take those and repeat the process on another page! The more you do this the better you get.

Here are the six simple steps to successful ideation:

1   Be clear about your purpose, like how to increase your profits, or perhaps planning a themed party.
2   Visualize a page (or pages) full of ideas.
3   Start writing.
4   Go fast—put down whatever comes to mind.
5   Do not judge any of it.
6   When you are finished, visualize; put pen to paper and start writing more. The "starting writing" will encourage more ideas to come forth.

ASSIGNMENT

Do at least one ideation session per week on various topics that either interest you or are part of your projects.

What if I'm still a bit skeptical?

Not to worry. I'm going to share a concept with you, which when you master it could change your life. First I'm going to ask you a possibly painful question. How many skills or ideas have you heard or experienced in your life that you felt would be of great benefit to you? How many of those are you not using on a consistent basis? Most people roll their eyes and let out a sigh. The fact is that we try things and then somehow lose track of them and forget them. Months or years can go by until we are reminded about them. We wonder what happened. We started out excited and eager to use them. Somewhere along the way they were lost. How did that happen?

One reason it happened is because we never really took these ideas to our hearts. They never became "second nature." Why? There are a couple of reasons. One possibility is that our "comfort zone" never expanded to embrace it. This is the part of the mind that accepts something as a normal part of who we are, that is consistent with who we believe we are at an unconscious level. Comfort zones cover many different areas of life: wealth, relationships, fashion, cars, praise, tidiness, noise, violence, humor, physical contact and many more.

Another reason we lose track of skills is that we tried them but they didn't work fast enough for us. Some things take time to master before we get the kinds of results we were promised. This is especially true if the skill in question is far outside our comfort zone! In fact, there is often a direct relationship between how far outside the zone it is and how good it would be for us.

It turns out that we must practice such new skills consistently over a long enough period of time for them to feel natural to us. Interestingly, the minimum number of days (the magical 21) it takes for something new in our life to feel normal is fairly cross-cultural. This concept was first put forward by Dr. Maxwell Maltz in his book *Psycho-cybernetics*, written in 1960.

Summary

- Give yourself a fair chance to master each skill.

- Set goals for the subjects and authors you want to read.

- Practice ideation on topics that interest you.

- Be patient and keep at it. Remember you need to practice your new skills over a long enough period of time that they feel like "second nature."

5.

Testing your reading effectiveness

Testing your abilities is one of the keystones to success in SuperReading™. This is done by checking your reading effectiveness (R.E.) level before starting the course and at intervals as you work your way through the book. That is what this chapter is about. Whenever you take a test you learn something about yourself that goes beyond the scores.

At one time the only reading comprehension tests available used multiple-choice questions to determine comprehension and recall. The "fill in the blank" tests I have devised are a far more accurate assessment of memory and comprehension skills. These tests are tough!

How to test yourself

The first thing you need to do is find out what your present reading effectiveness (R.E.) level is. You will be measuring both your speed and your comprehension/recall. You will do this by reading a 400-word essay and answering ten questions about it. Afterward, you will repeat the same steps again. At that point you will correct the tests, and look up your speed and R.E. on the tables in Appendix D. You will find one test in this chapter, and there are others in Appendix B.

When reading the test essay, please read it for comprehension. Do not try to go fast. Read at your normal speed, knowing there will be fill-in-the-blank questions to answer when you've finished. Do not look at the questions on the essay until you come to answer them. You will have to time yourself on the reading in minutes and seconds.

Read every word of the essay. Read through it once. When you are done, check your time. Immediately record your time. For example, if you take 2 minutes and 14 seconds; write down 2:14. Now move on to the questions. If you cannot recall an answer after about 20 seconds, let it go. How long would you keep trying to remember a fact in a conversation before moving on to the next point? When you have answered the ten questions, turn the page and read the essay a second time (time yourself again). When you are finished, record your time and then answer all the questions again.

When you read the essay for the second time, try to learn enough to get 100 percent on the re-test. (Remember that you only time your reading of the essay. You do NOT time yourself answering the questions.)

Remember:

- Do not look back at the essay when answering the questions
- Spelling doesn't matter in this instance
- Read through the essay once for the first test. Do not go back over it before answering the questions.

SUMMARY

- Read for comprehension.

- Time your reading for both test and re-test in minutes and seconds.

- It's not an "open book test"—you must recall your answers from memory.

- Questions are not timed.

Testing phobia

Do you tend to freeze up or get anxious when you take tests? Does the very word "test" fill you with dread? Do you feel wary when it comes to testing? If any of the above applies to you, relax! It's OK—really. Whatever happens on the tests is fine. Your scores will probably increase over time. As you realize that your reading ability is getting better, you will not mind testing so much. You may even find that you look forward to it. Whatever happens with the tests, it's all irrelevant compared to your daily reading abilities. Those will certainly improve whether the tests reflect that or not. Consider this: if you had a choice between having great reading skills and doing well on these tests, which would you choose? Of course, most people would choose having great reading skills. Having the tests confirm that is just icing on the cake. Relax and see what happens. Never let your test scores deter you from using the techniques. Also, do not become overconfident if your test scores skyrocket. That can be almost as dangerous as getting discouraged if they fall.

What about erratic scores?

Most of the time, you will find that your scores go up. However, that may not always be the case as there are many factors that can affect them adversely.

Why would they go up and down? There are a variety of reasons, including:

- your interest in the material
- how much sleep you've had
- whether or not you are eating a balanced diet
- your present stress levels
- the time of day
- the day of the week
- environmental distractions
- how many deadlines you have
- whether you are ill or becoming ill
- relationship challenges.

Or perhaps your scores dip because you are using a new skill or technique. Skills take time to develop and sometimes you may be using a relatively new skill that has not come to full power for you. If you have your eye on the big picture, a dip in your scores now and then is nothing to be concerned about.

If you do find your R.E. score has dropped, you can take more than one action. You can check to see that you are on track in learning and adopting new skills. You can go over the list of items that can interfere with reading. Or, you can simply think of it as a blip and look forward to an increase in your score in following tests.

I know that SuperReading™ is a rock-solid, logical reading improvement method. You *will* get better and better in your abilities. Always remember the big picture and don't worry about any temporary setbacks. You will rise above them and be brilliant.

Testing and English as a second language

If your first language is not English, your vocabulary may hold back your scores for a while. Be aware of this possibility as you take tests and perhaps see your scores go down once or twice. If your scores have been good and then suddenly dip, it may well be due to not understanding all the words in a particular essay. Stopping to work out the meaning of a word will count against you, as the clock is running and your reading time is half the formula for determining your reading effectiveness score. This is worth remembering because all the tests are on different subjects and you cannot tell in advance which ones may give you more of a vocabulary challenge.

If English is not your first language you should not get discouraged and remember that you need to keep your eye on the big picture even more than native English speakers.

Scoring yourself

Now that you know all about the theory behind testing, the next topic to look at before you embark upon the tests themselves is scoring. Remember that you do not score your tests until you have completed both the test and the re-test.

Here's how to score your tests:

1   When you get an answer totally correct, either in the test or the re-test, give yourself a score of 10.
2   Give yourself a zero when you get an answer wrong or leave it blank. Numerical answers must be totally correct or you score zero.
3   Score 5 for a partially correct answer. For example, if the correct answer is "Alexander Fleming," you get 5 points for "Fleming" and 10 points for "Alexander Fleming."
4   Add up your numbers—this gives you your comprehension score. For example, 70 points represents 70 percent comprehension.

5 Turn to Appendix D. In the left column of the table, look up the time you noted down for your reading, both for the test and then for the re-test. The number immediately to the right of your reading time is your words per minute (w.p.m.) score. Make a note of this.

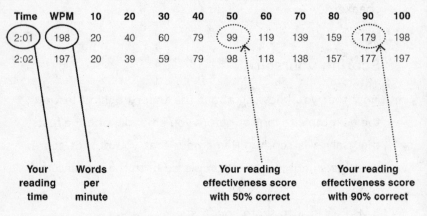

Time	WPM	10	20	30	40	50	60	70	80	90	100
2:01	198	20	40	60	79	99	119	139	159	179	198
2:02	197	20	39	59	79	98	118	138	157	177	197

Your reading time	Words per minute				Your reading effectiveness score with 50% correct				Your reading effectiveness score with 90% correct	

How to find your reading effectiveness (R.E.) score

6 The numbers across the top of the chart refer to your comprehension score, or number of correct answers. If, for example, you got five answers correct (5 x a score of 10), follow down the 50 column until it meets the row your time is on. The number where the column and row meet is your reading effectiveness (R.E.) score. If your score on a test is an odd number, such as 75, then your R.E. score would be the figure between 70 and 80. You will need to calculate that for yourself.

For example, if your reading time was 2 minutes and 4 seconds and you scored 75 points, your R.E. score would be halfway between 135 and 155, i.e. 145.

You can test yourself either once a week or fortnightly. After you have worked through all the techniques in the book (this should take from six to eight weeks) you can test yourself monthly or even quarterly. Once a test has been read you should not use it again. Although, after you have followed the steps in this book, you would be surprised at how little you recall from your first tests, because your skills were low at the beginning.

Reading test 1

The first test follows. Further tests are in Appendix B and you can take them in any order. You will need a stopwatch (to count minutes and seconds) and a pen or pencil. Start your stopwatch; then begin to read. No note taking!

Test 1: Biography of George Stephenson

George Stephenson was a British engineer who designed a famous and historically important steam-powered locomotive named Rocket. He is known as the father of British steam railways.

George Stephenson was born in Wylam, England,

west of Newcastle upon Tyne. Stephenson grew up near the Wylam coal mine, and in 1802 began working there as an engineman. For ten years his knowledge of steam engines increased, until in 1812 he stopped operating them for a living, and started building them.

Stephenson designed his first locomotive in 1814, a traveling engine designed for hauling coal. Named Blucher, it could haul 30 tons of coal in a load, and was the first successful flanged-wheel locomotive. That means it was the first locomotive to use flanged wheels to rest on the track. Over the next five years, he built sixteen more engines.

As his success grew, Stephenson was hired to build an 8-mile railway from Hetton to Sunderland. The finished line used a combination of gravity pulling the load down inclines and locomotives for level and uphill stretches. It was the first ever railway to use no animal power at all.

In 1821, a project began to build the Stockton and Darlington Railway. Originally the plan was to use horses to draw coal carts over metal rails. Stephenson convinced company director Edward Pease to change the plans. Three years later Stephenson completed the first locomotive for the new railroad. It was at first named Active, but later renamed Locomotion. Driven by Stephenson himself, Locomotion hauled an 80-ton load of coal and flour for nine miles, reaching a top speed of 24 miles per hour. The first purpose-built passenger carriage, dubbed Experiment, was also attached, and held a load of dignitaries for the opening journey. It was the first time passenger traffic had ever been run on a steam-driven locomotive railway.

While building the S&D line, Stephenson had noticed that even small inclines significantly reduced the speed of the locomotives. Even slight declines made the primitive brakes almost useless. He concluded that railways should be kept as level as possible. On future railways he executed a series of difficult cuts, embankments and stone viaducts to smooth the route.

As the Liverpool and Manchester line approached completion in 1829, a competition was held to decide who would build the locomotives. Stephenson's entry was Rocket, and its impressive victory made it the most famous machine in the world.

Note down your reading time; then answer the questions on the next page:

TIME ....

QUESTIONS

Biography of George Stephenson

1. In what city was Stephenson born?
2. How long did Stephenson work at the coal mine?
3. What was the name of Stephenson's first locomotive?
4. What kind of wheels did his first locomotive have?
5. On the Hetton to Sunderland line, what did Stephenson use for pulling loads down declines?
6. Who was director of the Stockton and Darlington
   Railway?
7. Stephenson named an engine Active. Later, the name
   was changed to what?
8. What was the name of the first passenger carriage
   run on a steam railway?
9. Name one feature Stephenson used after building
   the Stockton and Darlington line to keep the railways
   level.
10. What was the name of the most famous machine in
    the world (at that time)?

Now go to the next page and read the article again.

Time yourself!

Test 1: Biography of George Stephenson

George Stephenson was a British engineer who designed a famous and historically important steam-powered locomotive named Rocket. He is known as the father of British steam railways.

George Stephenson was born in Wylam, England, west of Newcastle upon Tyne. Stephenson grew up near the Wylam coal mine, and in 1802 began working there as an engineman. For ten years his knowledge of steam engines increased, until in 1812 he stopped operating them for a living, and started building them.

Stephenson designed his first locomotive in 1814, a traveling engine designed for hauling coal. Named Blucher, it could haul 30 tons of coal in a load, and was the first successful flanged-wheel locomotive. That means it was the first locomotive to use flanged wheels to rest on the track. Over the next five years, he built sixteen more engines.

As his success grew, Stephenson was hired to build an 8-mile railway from Hetton to Sunderland. The finished line used a combination of gravity pulling the load down inclines and locomotives for level and uphill stretches. It was the first ever railway to use no animal power at all.

In 1821, a project began to build the Stockton and Darlington Railway. Originally the plan was to use horses to draw coal carts over metal rails. Stephenson convinced company director Edward Pease to change the plans. Three years later Stephenson completed the first locomotive for the new railroad. It was at first named Active, but later renamed Locomotion. Driven by Stephenson himself, Locomotion hauled an 80-ton load of coal and flour for nine miles, reaching a top speed of 24 miles per hour. The first purpose-built passenger carriage, dubbed Experiment, was also attached, and held a load of dignitaries for the opening journey. It was the first time passenger traffic had ever been run on a steam-driven locomotive railway.

While building the S&D line, Stephenson had noticed that even small inclines significantly reduced the speed of the locomotives. Even slight declines made the primitive brakes almost useless. He concluded that railways should be kept as level as possible. On future railways he executed a series of difficult cuts, embankments and stone viaducts to smooth the route.

As the Liverpool and Manchester line approached completion in 1829, a competition was held to decide who would build the locomotives. Stephenson's entry was Rocket, and its impressive victory made it the most famous machine in the world.

Note down your reading time; then answer the questions on the next page:

TIME ....

QUESTIONS

Biography of George Stephenson

1. In what city was Stephenson born?
2. How long did Stephenson work at the coal mine?
3. What was the name of Stephenson's first locomotive?
4. What kind of wheels did his first locomotive have?
5. On the Hetton to Sunderland line, what did Stephenson use for pulling loads down declines?
6. Who was director of the Stockton and Darlington Railway?
7. Stephenson named an engine Active. Later, the name was changed to what?
8. What was the name of the first passenger carriage run on a steam railway?
9. Name one feature Stephenson used after building the Stockton and Darlington line to keep the railways level.
10. What was the name of the most famous machine in the world (at that time)?

Now go to page 301 in Appendix B and get the answers.

Grade yourself! On page 322 there is a graph on which you can record your scores so you can chart your improvement over time at a glance.

If your score was low, don't despair. *How to Be a Super-Reader* will help you improve.

The personal testing method

I also recommend testing yourself in a less formal manner. Using reading material that you read often, like a journal, book or other source, time yourself reading for a specific number of minutes (from three to eight). Then put the reading material aside and write down everything you remember from the text. Then count the number of lines you read and write that on your answer sheet. Revisit similar material six weeks later and read for the same amount of time. Just make sure there is more material there than today, because you will get further than you did today. You could do this every two weeks, or however often you wish. I'm certain you will be pleased with the results, assuming you followed the recipe for reading success.

ASSIGNMENT

Test yourself using the personal testing method every six weeks.

SUMMARY

- Testing is not absolutely necessary but it is highly recommended because it can show that you are making progress.

- If you test yourself, you will begin to "normal-ize" your top speed, comprehension and recall, meaning that it will get better and you will "forget" how bad it was before.

- Do remember that scores can drop for all sorts of reasons, from stress to lack of interest in the subject. Do not get disheartened!

- If you feel you did very badly, remember the big picture. Soon you will be a super reader. It's only a matter of time.

PART TWO:

Your New Basic Reading Technique

6.

Introducing
hand pacing

Now begins your journey through the skills that will turn you into a super reader. The following chapters outline and detail the techniques you will need to learn and use, and are really the "How to" part of the book. You will be covering hand pacing (in this chapter), previewing (chapter 7) and learning to read multiple words at a glance (chapter 8). From this point on, you will be altering your behavior, and this will improve your results. This is where your positive "can-do" attitude and belief will harness the power of your brain and improve your ability to read, retain and remember written information.

After each new tool is introduced, I suggest a reading assignment to give you the opportunity to practice your new skill. Remember that sometimes new skills may cause a temporary drop in performance. This is because you are not only performing the new technique, you are also thinking about how you are doing it. That splits your attention for a little while. Don't worry. Your ability will pick back up again and surpass what it was before.

Are you ready to leave old habits behind and move forward with simple, powerful techniques? If your answer is yes, then let's proceed.

First things first. Before you start reading, you need to think about how you are sitting.

Are you sitting comfortably?

You may not realize this, but the way you sit affects your reading ability. If you are like most people, you probably just pull your chair up to a table and start reading. Before you do that, I would like you to turn your chair 45 degrees, allowing your elbow to rest on the table. If you are right-handed, please rotate your chair to the left, or counter-clockwise, and rest your right elbow on the table. If you are left-handed, swivel your chair to the right, or clock-wise, and rest your left elbow. (See the illustrations on the next page.)

Now, hold your book with your free hand, either flat on the desk or propped up to about 30 or 40 degrees to bring the text to a friendlier angle for your eyes. You can prop it up with some books or anything that brings up the far edge about 2 or 3 inches. Be relaxed, and swiveling left and right from your elbow, you will use your finger to follow the lines as you read the paragraph that follows. When you read, go as fast as you can **with** comprehension.

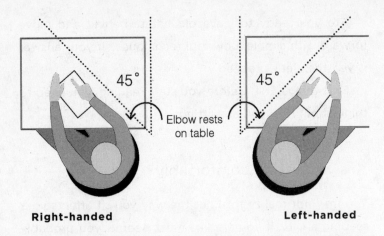

Right-handed   **Left-handed**

For most people, sitting like this is very natural and easy. And if it does not feel natural, it will very soon. Sometimes it takes a few minutes because you are doing several new things at once. Do not judge yourself or these techniques harshly. Be patient. Even people with the most negative attitudes only take a day or two to get used to it. For most people, within a week they can't imagine going back to reading "the old way." At first, you will not only be reading, you will also be thinking about pointing and pacing (you will learn all about this in the rest of this chapter). This may even distract you from the meaning of the words. This newness will wear off and soon you will ignore your finger and how you're seated and focus on the words. Do you understand this paragraph? If so, you are doing just fine. If you are totally lost, just keep reserving judgment (see chapter 4), until you get it.

Hand pacing

When I'm teaching the SuperReading™ course, I get everyone's attention and then throw a soft object the length of
the room. I then ask who watched the object. Everyone
raises their hand. Then I ask whether they made a conscious
decision to watch it or if it was more a reflex. Virtually everyone agrees it's a reflex, as there's little time to make a
considered decision. Why is this important? Because I want
you to understand that the tool you are about to learn is
well thought out. It makes sense and works very, very well.
It is one of the foundations of this program.

So why did I ask about watching the object? I asked
because it is natural for humans to pay attention to
a moving object. All animals do. It's natural because that
moving object might be a predator come to eat us. Our
ancestors had to watch out for all sorts of nasty beasts like
lions and tigers and snakes and scorpions and who knows
what. Those who paid attention to movement lived. There
is a technical term for those people who did not pay attention to moving objects: lunch! We can use this natural
reflex to our advantage.

If you are right-handed, raise your right hand. Left-
handers raise your left. Now point to the sky.

 That forefinger doing the pointing is your new
reading tool! Use it to pace yourself as you read.
Do this by moving it under the words you are
reading in a smooth, fluid motion. Most children

in societies with written languages often use their fingers to keep their place as they read. Most educators have been told to "correct" this tendency. Funny, but it turns out that using the hand is a natural, intuitive technique that works very well with the right tools. You're now getting those tools.

Hand pacing is quite wonderful. When I ask graduates even years after they have finished the SuperReading™ course, hand pacing is always one of their top three tools. Without hand pacing, they say, their minds wander off and they waste untold hours of their precious time. It also stops them reading the same sentence again and again before they understand the meaning.

ASSIGNMENT

Put up several small cards around your computer and other places with the word "POINT!" written on them. Change them around every couple of days so they continue to catch your eye.

When you are hand pacing, you may speed up or slow down, depending on the material you are reading. However, while reading, remember to keep your hand moving! Do not stop. At first, you may miss some things. That's OK. Your brain is capable of processing at rates many times faster than you do now. It will also get lazy if you let it. Let your brain know that it must process what you read as you go. It is very capable of this, and will quickly learn how to remember what you have read. However, you must give it no alternative. If you miss something, let it go. You can pick it up later when you "review" (see chapter 10).

From this point forward, you will track underneath the line you are reading and remember the basic rule of hand pacing:

> GO AS FAST AS YOU CAN WHILE MAINTAINING
> COMPREHENSION.

ASSIGNMENT

Read the following four paragraphs using your finger. Just trace underneath each line. Remember that you are in control of your speed. Match your speed to your comprehension. **Begin.**

This will mean more to you than ever before. Do you remember when we talked about "distracted reader syndrome" earlier? That's when you're reading along, thinking you're absorbing the material and then when you get to the end you realize (with horror) that you have almost no idea of what you read. Usually, the distraction is coming from within your head. You start daydreaming. Why? Well, let's face it; movies tend to be more fun than articles, reports or textbooks. That's what your brain was doing—running movies while it fooled you into thinking you were reading!

Remember when you learned how to read when you were at school? The teacher probably got you to read aloud to make sure you could do it. Once you demonstrated the ability to "decode" the words, your teacher probably told you to keep reading silently to yourself. The problem with this was that you were only reading silently as far as the outside world could tell, but inside your head you were still pronouncing the words (sub-vocalizing). That set up two barriers for you. One was that you could not read much faster than you could talk. That is called the sub-vocalization barrier, which is to reading what the sound barrier is to flight. The other was that at some point your brain learned that if it pronounced the words, you believed you were reading. Eventually it had you saying the words but it stopped processing them—or at least not very deeply. At that point you experienced distracted reader syndrome.

In fact, if you've ever studied and learned to read a foreign language you will know this feeling. You can read that other language, sometimes quite well, without understanding a single thing you read! For instance, I'm a bit rusty in Spanish, but I can read it rather nicely. The only problem is I have almost no idea of what I'm saying.

For the first time in years you will know whether you are understanding what you are reading or not. Pointing at what you read gives that to you. It sets up a circuit between your brain and the material. If the circuit is broken you become aware of it immediately. Specifically, if what you're pointing at does not match up with what you're thinking about, the difference becomes obvious.

So how was that? Did reading along with your finger feel natural? Did it feel weird? Did it feel good? Did it get better as you went along? Are you still reading with your finger? Did you have a performance dip, or was it OK? Whatever your reaction now, in the big picture it does not matter too much. Soon you will read with accuracy and good comprehension. If it was a bit off then you will get better at it very soon.

Keep reading with your finger from now on. This is just about the most important technique in the book. Whatever you've heard about pointing at what you read, it is the single best tool for high comprehension, focus and concentration.

The flip turn

When you are reading along, using your finger to trace under the line, it's important to keep a good pace going. While you should not sacrifice comprehension for a steady pace, there is something to be said for keeping the brain active and focused. When it comes to efficiency with your time, the flip turn is important on multiple levels.

When I was researching reading techniques I went to libraries and parks to observe people reading, without their knowledge. If they had known they were being observed they would have behaved differently. I needed to know what people do naturally when they read, and how long it took them to do it.

I would sit or stand casually nearby, and when they turned a page I noted the time or started a stopwatch. I could usually tell when they flipped a page, and could almost always tell when they went from the left page to the right page by their head or eye movement. It usually took them between 90 seconds and 120 seconds per page. Sometimes I would walk by to see the titles of the books, and later I would go to a bookshop and look at the books to get an idea of how many words were on a page. Sometimes I would go up to people and ask them to show me the book as it looked interesting. When they showed me, I would quickly count the number of lines where they had been reading.

I began to notice, and this was something I was previously unaware of, how long it sometimes took people to turn the page when they were finished with the right-hand page. Usually they would turn the page fairly quickly in just a second or two. However, sometimes they could not quite grab it and would have to try several times to get traction. Often they would have to wet their finger to grip the page and turn it. This process could take anywhere from 3 seconds up to nearly 10 seconds if they were in no particular hurry. The average was about 4 seconds, which may not sound like much. Indeed, if you're taking upward of 2 minutes (120 seconds) to read a page, then I will admit that 4 seconds is not much time. It's only 3 percent of the time spent reading that page. But what if you are becoming a super reader? What if eventually you are reading a similar page in 20 to 25 seconds instead of 120 seconds? Now, turning the page is taking upward of 20 percent of your reading time on that page, which is a lot of time for your finger to be flicking a page corner. This is not a productive use of your time.

The solution is simple. As your reading finger clears the first few lines of the right-hand page, move your other hand across and prepare the page for turning. It's poised to turn the page when you get to the bottom. The result? When your reading finger finishes the last word on the page, your other hand flips the page over and your reading finger comes down at the top left and picks up where you left off without missing a beat. It's a smooth, fluid motion; just like Olympic swimmers do when they get to the end of the pool. They flip over and push off the wall for power. You are doing the same thing with your reading!

When I watch people reading in my classes I have

often noticed that when people get to the bottom of a right-hand page, they hesitate and look back over the text a bit before turning the page. To me this means they do not believe they have absorbed the material. I want you to trust yourself. If you have previewed (chapter 7) and are pointing using hand pacing, you are getting loads of information. The time to find out is when you parrot (chapter 9). Furthermore, there is not usually anything that special at the bottom of the page. I do not observe people doing this on any other part of a page—only on the bottom right-hand side. This tells me quite clearly the readers are looking at this as their last chance to get it right on those two pages before turning. Since we have a review step built into our reading (chapter 10), we do not need to do that. We can continue with confidence that we are getting what we need, and if not we will check in at the proper time to assess our reading.

Remember that whatever information is on the last line of the right-hand page is only there by happenstance, depending on the size of the font and the amount of space between the lines. Therefore, dwelling on it is artificial. So I'm asking you to keep going when you get to the bottom, do the flip turn and keep reading on the next page.

READING IN BED

I'm often asked about whether it's OK to read in bed. I have some strong thoughts on this subject. The answer is: yes and no. I know there are few things in this world as nice as curling up under the cover with a great book. What you want to be careful about, however, is creating subsequent effects from that. Ivan Pavlov conducted one of the most famous experiments in history in the early 20th century, coming up with the concept of classical conditioning. He had a collection of dogs. He would ring a bell, and then bring them some meat. Ring the bell, bring the meat. It didn't take long for the dogs to associate the ringing bell with the meat. After a few times, ringing the bell would start the dogs salivating. They had become conditioned to respond to the bell. They would also generalize to other similar sounds.

My concern is that your body becomes conditioned to getting sleepy when you read. If the pattern is: read, feel drowsy, read, feel drowsy, read, feel drowsy, then that can cause a problem. The worst case is when people like to read in order to fall asleep. If you must read in bed, put the book down at the very first sign of drowsiness. Do not carry on into nearly falling asleep. My students who have stopped reading in bed report that they no longer feel drowsy when they read during the day. My suggestion is to try it for 21 days in a row (or as often as you read in bed) and see the difference. The choice is yours. My job is to provide the tools and the means to test them.

ASSIGNMENT

Avoid reading in bed for either 21 days or 21 times (if you don't read to fall asleep every night). Do you notice the difference during the day when you read?

Reading from a computer screen

If you don't like reading from a computer screen and prefer to print documents out, try the following techniques for at least 21 days. Most people find that when they learn the skills of SuperReading™ they are able to read from a computer screen more successfully, especially if they have a positive attitude. If you make up your mind to have a good time with your improved skills, you will reap more benefit than if you look out for what might go wrong.

When you read from a computer screen, use the mouse cursor. It will not follow along as precisely as your finger on paper, but it will be close enough to keep your attention focused on where you wish to be. If you don't currently have a mouse with your computer, consider investing in a small USB mouse, which may be easier to use than running your finger along the words on the screen.

The position of your computer screen

The latest advice is to have the top of your computer screen just below eye level, especially if you tend to lean forward. Try leaning forward while keeping your eyes level. Notice how you tend to compress the vertebrae in your neck. That is not good for your health! For the latest research, look up "computer ergonomics" (also known as human engineering) in a search engine for more information.

Positioning your computer screen for hand pacing

Most computers are not well positioned for reading using the hand pacing method. Here are the various options:

1 Use the mouse cursor to move along the line to keep you focused. It will not be a perfectly straight line, but it will do.
2 Get a desk that allows you to place the monitor within the desktop. Such desks have a hole cut into the top of the desk with a suspended, adjustable mount for your monitor. Use your finger on the screen. This should only be done for short periods of time, as it's difficult to properly support your arm and shoulder.

3   With LCD monitors you can really fly if they quickly dismount from their stand and sit right on your lap or the desk. You would have one finger on the screen and the other finger on the Page Down key or mouse wheel. It's the ideal option, though more expensive. You have to figure what your time is worth per hour and compare that to the cost of the monitor. The time to make such a decision is once you're competent with pattern reading (see chapter 11).

4   Tablets lie flat and can be used in either portrait or landscape mode. Their screens can rotate and flip over and around as well. They function like an electronic book and are excellent for fun and efficient reading. They are a bit more expensive but worth it if you plan on doing a lot of reading.

How to set up the text on your screen

Whatever kind of screen you are reading, find a way to narrow the columns of text. Make them as much like newspaper columns as possible. If the application has word wrap, simply grab the sides of the text and narrow it. The extra few seconds taken to arrange the page are well worth it for the speed and comprehension you gain. In MS Word, click View, then Web Layout to get word wrap. Now you can grab the side of the window and drag it to make the window narrower without losing any of the words. Make the line hold about eight to ten words across on average. This does not have to be precise, just approximate.

Remember that making the column narrower results in a document that has more pages. The amount of content is the same, but the document is now physically "longer." I bring this up because the apparent size of a document has a psychological effect on the reader. If someone hands you a two-page report, that feels different from being handed a 200-page report. Our reaction is totally different when the only difference is the length. You may experience something similar when you narrow the columns. Suddenly a three-page document is a ten-page document! Do not be fooled by that illusion. Just because you're hitting the Page Down key more often, you will be reading through it faster because the information is in bite-sized chunks!

Also be aware of the font size. The smaller the font the more likely it is that you will have to lean forward to see it clearly. That compresses the vertebrae in your neck and can cause health problems. The solution is either to change the font size or the percentage of magnification on the page. In an MS Word document, that drop down menu is located in View. You can either choose a predetermined value (100%, 150%, 200%) or left-click the number and type in your own value.

| Words words words
words words words
words words words
words words words
words words words
words words words
words words words
words words words
words words words
words words words
words words words
words words words | Words words words words words words words words
words words words words words words words words
words words words words words words words words
words words words words words words words words
words words words words words words words words
words words words words words words words words
words words words words words words words words
words words words words words words words words
words words words words words words words words
words words words words words words words words
words words words words words words words words
words words words words words words words words |

Narrow column   **Wide column**

The ideal would be to get just the right number of words across your column as you can read in one or two glances. This will be looked at in more detail when you learn about Eye-Hop™ in chapter 8. As you progress in your Eye-Hop™ practice, you can use wider and wider columns.

The color of the screen

Near-sightedness (or short-sightedness) is rising in the world. Some experts believe this may be due to squinting into brightly lit monitors and changing the shape of our eyeballs. At the least, looking at a bright monitor screen is going to be tiring on the eyes. In old films, the police would always shine a bright light at a suspect when questioning them. This was so uncomfortable that they would always confess. So why are we torturing ourselves when we read?

The answer is to either turn down the brightness or

change the background color. You can do this in less than
a minute. With Windows XP:

Click START
Control Panel /
Display /
Appearance /
Advanced /
Click on Window Text / Color 1 /

Then use the drop down menu to choose a light blue
or light green (possibly very light pink).
Click OK

This will change the background color in all of your
applications, but the color will not print out. It only affects
your viewing panel. I have suggested a light color because
you still need contrast between the background and your
text. If they are too close in value you will still be squinting
to read and will have defeated your purpose!

ASSIGNMENT

Once you have set up your screen correctly and sorted
out the appearance of your text, get a document up on
your screen. Use the mouse cursor to read along. It does
not matter whether you move the cursor under the
line or on the line. Do it whichever way feels comfortable. Unlike your finger, the cursor is almost invisible

and does not interfere with seeing the words. When I first started to teach this course in 1995, about one-third of the students were uncomfortable using the cursor to track along. As society has become more familiar with using computers, most people just adapt to it in a couple of days. If for some reason you take longer to adapt, remember the 21-day rule for adopting a new habit and look back to chapter 4 on reserving judgment.

SUMMARY

- Use your basic hand pacing technique from now on. A good attitude toward using your finger will make the transition from using only your eyes much easier. At some point, you will be completely used to this lifestyle change and it will be second nature for you.

- Sitting comfortably will make reading for long periods more tolerable. If a table or desk is not available and you are sitting in a chair, prop your forearms against your side. A pillow or two under the book will keep it at a comfortable distance from your eyes.

- Go as fast as you can while maintaining comprehension. Remember—comprehension is king!

- The flip turn will help your flow, and it is good psychologically. Knowing you are heading for it, and later practicing it at speed, is proof that you've become a super reader.

- Reading in bed is not advised if it makes your eyes tired. You may be sacrificing good attention the next day.

- Reading from the computer screen is part of life, so make sure all that time spent is not at the expense of your physical well-being. Make sure you follow the latest hints and best practices for good ergonomics.

7.

Previewing

Once you have come to grips with hand pacing, and are comfortable with using your finger (or cursor) to track your reading, you are ready to move on to previewing, one of the other top three techniques in this book. When taking the first reading test in chapter 5, you will probably have noticed how much easier it was to answer the questions after reading the text for the second time. This is because you were familiar with the information. You understood what it was about, who was involved and for what purpose. You may have remembered some facts and they made more sense the second time through. You could say that you "previewed" the essay with your first read. However, you can do better than that. There are special strategies that can give you loads of good information without having to read all the text the first time. These strategies are called "previewing."

Previewing lets you know what's coming. It's a strategic way to get a peek ahead at what you will be reading. It serves some of the same functions as a movie preview. When you watch a preview, or trailer, it shows you enough of the movie to get you interested. One difference is that the movie preview doesn't give away too much. Previewing when you read can give you loads of valuable information.

There are three main ways to preview: key sentence previewing; name and number scan; and novel previewing. The first technique is usually people's favorite. It's the one that is used about 90 percent of the time.

Key sentence previewing

Key sentence previewing is quite simple. Read the first sentence of each paragraph. Most authors load a lot of information into the first sentence. Try to only preview the first five to ten pages or so, if there are long chapters. It's hard to keep much more information in your head, especially when you're just starting off. The rule is to key sentence preview only as much as you can accurately recall.

> **ASSIGNMENT**
>
> Test your present abilities by reading five key sentences from a book and discovering how much you can recall from those. If you get them all, try to do more until you get a significant drop-off in your recall. It's like body building—each time you push yourself, you grow stronger. If right now you can recall four key sentences,

work on that for a couple of days. Then work at mastering five. Then six, and so on.

After reading the key sentences, try forming mental pictures of each point as you go. It's OK to be outrageous. Mental pictures are a clever way to remember information. Pictures have far more power than most words and are usually far easier to remember. They trigger different parts of the brain, which use more imagination. When you make mental pictures, make them larger than life, with color and sound if possible. The more ways you can hook into the concept you wish to remember, the more likely you will remember it. For instance, you can say the thing you want to remember several times while visualizing (see more on this in chapter 12). This will conjure up your internal mental image, making the connection more complete.

As your mind strengthens, keep raising the bar. Between your brain stretching to keep up and the new techniques you will learn throughout the rest of this book, your abilities will grow. Once you have read the prescribed number of key sentences, be that ten or more, go back to where you started key sentence previewing and read all the words, including the key sentences, again. The double exposure will help your retention. Repetition is one of the five important keys to memory (there is more on this in chapter 13). Try the following fun test, which proves that repetition is a great way to learn.

Key sentence previewing

What is 6 x 6?

Did you get the answer right away?

Let's try another one.

What is 3 x 3?

Did you have to think hard? Did you have to put a hand to your head and close your eyes to concentrate and draw numbers in the air to figure it out? No? The answer just popped into your head, right?

OK, let's try something different. This time, when you look, try NOT to let the answer pop into your head. Ready?

What is 5 x 5?

The answer just popped into your head. That was easy.

You may have squeezed it out by thinking of something else, but it was right there for you, all ready and very accurate. No hard thinking—all it needed was mentioning. Don't you sometimes wish you could remember everything that easily? What made the answer come up so quickly? The answer is repetition. Years ago you learned the multiplication tables by sheer repetition, and still they pop up effortlessly. That's how powerful repetition is for learning. Fortunately, there are other methods for effective learning besides repetition. We will be exploring them in this book. For now, let's really drive the point home. Let's try one more case from the multiplication tables.

What is the answer to 17 x 17?

Hmmm. You don't get the same response from your brain now, do you? What happened? 17 x 17 was on the table, but you probably didn't spend as much time learning it. Therefore nothing sprang to mind when you looked at it. You saw the answer years ago, so you understand the concept and just after looking at it could have given the correct answer (which is 289, by the way). However, one look does not put the answer into your long-term memory, does it? That would take another one of the five keys to memory—namely emotion. If the last time you looked at 17 x 17 something highly emotional happened, you would probably remember it. Emotion seals in memories, but more on that when we get to it in chapter 13.

CASE STUDY

I once taught a group of teachers, one of whom was attending university at night. He was also working part-time somewhere else! After our second class, he went home and discovered that he had a test in two hours for which he hadn't even opened the book! Worse, it was in a required subject he had little interest in! The test covered the first hundred pages. He cracked open the binding (for the first time), and began doing key sentence preview. By the time he had to leave for the test, he had covered only sixty pages. He ended up getting 80 percent in the exam! Would you say there's a lot of important information in those key sentences? He certainly did.

Alpha-omega—a special case of key sentence previewing

Alpha-omega means "first and last" and refers to the beginning and ending paragraphs of an article or piece of writing. In a typical news story, for example, the first two paragraphs are supposed to tell you the "who, what, when and where" of the article. Usually, the last paragraph is a summary of the article and is used to drive home the author's point, or "why." By reading the alpha-omega, you do at least two things: one, you have an excellent idea of what the story is all about, including the author's viewpoint; two, you can save a lot of time if this article does not interest you, based on what the main points are. You can parrot what you have read (see chapter 9).

Occasionally you come across an author whose writing style is a bit different. They put important information not only in the first sentence of each paragraph, but also in the last sentence of each paragraph. With these authors you may want to do alpha-omega on each paragraph as a means of previewing and/or reviewing (chapter 10).

You can also use alpha-omega with a whole book as a way of getting a quick overview of it. The alpha in this case is the front cover and front jacket flap, while the omega is the back cover and back jacket flap. Some people like to include the preface and table of contents as part of their alpha-omega. Either is fine. The idea is to preview the book so you know the basic plot, some of the characters and the author's point of view. Remember the old saying, "You can't tell a book by its cover"? That is partially true. You can tell a few things about a book from its cover by using alpha-omega, but remember to keep your mind open as there will be more to it than meets the eye. I have met people who refuse to read some books because they contain ideas with which the reader does not agree. You are developing powerful tools of comprehension, so I suggest that it is OK to read such books. Just because you read it does not mean you have to believe it. Aristotle said it best: "It is the mark of an educated mind to be able to entertain a thought without accepting it." They will probably reinforce what you already believe. Just let go of your fears and don't believe everything you read.

The bookmark preview

You can also use alpha-omega in a different way. You use a bookmark and go through an entire book looking for items of interest. Spending no more than five seconds per page, every time you come across an item you are interested in learning more about, you jot the page number down on the back of a bookmark. You go through the whole book in 15 minutes or less and have specific targets you know will be of interest to you. Keep the bookmark with that book, as it is now dedicated to the best hot spots of information. If the information in the book is of particular importance to you, because of your career, a vocation or education, you may want to take notes as you preview for later reference. You may well be able to bookmark around 30 to 40 places in the book that appear to be of high interest. Those that turn out to be real gems can be circled to make them stand out. You can even write a word next to them to remind you of the topic. Although the bookmark could become separated and lost from the book, this technique will particularly satisfy those people who feel it is horrible to mark a book directly or fold page corners to mark a place. Some people are not that attached to their books, some think marking their books makes them theirs, and others would not dream of "damaging" a book.

Later in this book you will learn about a particularly useful note-taking method called Info-Mapping™, which will help you take notes for particularly easy reference and memory.

Name and number scan

Name and number scan

The second previewing technique is name and number scan. This is really suited to historical texts and research papers or any texts that are full of facts. Newspaper articles often have many facts in them. Scanning through them to pick up the who, what, when and where will give you the facts. Reading the full text will fill in the blanks. When you start to read, move your finger quickly down the page in a zigzag, looking for any names, such as those of people and places. Scan also for any numbers, such as dates, money, weights or how many of something there are. In either case, pause momentarily and make a mental note of the name or number. You can use the power of repetition and say the fact a few times. When you actually go back and read, you can fill in what the name or number was and why it was significant.

Becoming aware of all the facts in an essay or article can make you curious about how they all fit together. You may be wondering how 1887, the moon, Cambridge University and China all fit together. A curious mind works far better than a bored mind. Your brain holds on to all the puzzle pieces until they make sense. Holding on to them makes them remain in your memory longer.

ASSIGNMENT

Get a book that is likely to have a lot of names or dates or places. Scan down a few of the pages with your finger, looking for the name and number facts. Stop on each one for a couple of seconds. You can even say them aloud if you like. Then go back and read one of the pages. You will begin to notice how those facts jump back out at you. You will also notice how they tend to "stick" a bit better in your memory. They will make more sense once you get the context of how they fit together.

Novel previewing

The third technique is particularly apt for reading novels, although it can be used with any material, particularly where the targeting of the writing is not easy or obvious. With key sentence previewing, it's fairly obvious where the key words are. Name and number scan works well when there are lots of facts sprinkled through the text. Novel previewing fills up the void the other two techniques leave behind when they are not ideal. In theory, you could use novel previewing all the time, except that the other two techniques are specialized for when the author has either placed their key information in the key sentences or distributed facts all through the text.

Some good news is that reading your novels more quickly, with the right tools, will greatly enhance your experience. They will happen more at the speed of real life. In a book it takes you 90 seconds to read about how beautiful a garden is. In real life you know it in a second or two. As a super reader you'll know in about 12 seconds. This will feel better because that's closer to how you really experience your life. Novel previewing is a great tool if you are taking a literature course. It will give you a really good feel for what is in the book, while adding to your understanding and recall.

Novels require a technique that is quite different from that needed for textbooks, magazines and many other forms of the written word. The reason is that novels often have something other books don't have. Read the sample below (don't forget to use your finger!):

> Dr. Jones walked up to the old man. "Have you seen James?"
>
> "No, not since early this morning."
>
> "Was he here?"
>
> "No. He was at the hotel."
>
> "The hotel where I'm staying?"
>
> "Where are you staying?"
>
> "I'm at the Fairmont."
>
> "No, he was at the Lawrence Towers."
>
> "Was his wife with him?"
>
> "Yes. She looked younger than I remembered."
>
> "Yeah, surgery will do that."
>
> "Shall I tell James you were looking for him?"
>
> "No. I have a little surprize for him."

How is this different from other forms of writing? Novels have fewer paragraphs because they often have a lot of dialogue. As a result, key sentence previewing doesn't work as well for previewing novels. You need a different tool. You need novel previewing. It's quite simple and works remarkably well. In fact, you can use it for almost any text, though when there are paragraphs key sentence previewing is usually best.

Words words words words words words words words
words words words words words words words words
words words words words words words words words
words words words words words words **Sir Richard
ordered the fleet to attack.** words words words words
words words words words words words words words
Words words words words words words words words
words words words words words words words words
words words words words words words words words
words words words words words words words words
words words words words words words words words
words words words words words words words words
words words words words words words words words
words words words words words words words words
words words words words words words words words
words words words words words words words words
words words words words words words words words
words words words words words words words words
words words words words words words
words words words words words words words words
words words words **Their ship sank without a trace.**
Words words words words words words words words
words words words words words words words words
words words words words words words words words
words words words words words words words words
words words words words words words words words
words words words words words words words words
words words words words words words words words
words words words words words words words words

Novel previewing

Here's how novel previewing works. Simply drop down one-third of the page, read a line or two, drop another one-third, and read a line or two. Read just enough to get the idea of what's happening on that part of the page. You can also drop down by quarters, sampling three places on the page. This would be good to do when there is dense text with lots of words on the page. You will be amazed at how much of the story comes together for you.

> **ASSIGNMENT**
>
> Pick up a novel. Use novel previewing, dropping down a third, on a few pages. At first you can do three places per page. Just read enough to get the idea. Then write down what you remember. Now go back and read the pages. Compare how much was there with how much you picked up from the novel previewing. Usually the novel previewing technique gives you a fairly clear picture of what was happening on that page.

Students always worry whether novel previewing and therefore reading novels more quickly will spoil their enjoyment. The answer, of course, is no. First of all, you are free to read at any speed you like. You can speed up or slow down at your discretion, just like you've always done. The difference is that your range will be far wider. To me, the joy of a good book is that I get lost in it. I lose track of time and find myself immersed in this other world. When I stop, I have no idea of the time. One of the marks of having fun is losing track of time. Imagine laughing and laughing with your friends. Everyone's getting along and you feel great, and you have no idea how late it is. Were you all talking fast or slowly? Do you care? Does it matter? It's the same with reading. When you're fully into a book you have no idea whether you're reading quickly or not. You are probably reading faster than "normal" because you know the subject, you like the characters and you can't wait to see what will happen next.

The question is, so what if you're reading even faster

than that? The book will end eventually. Maybe the author will write more! You may as well have some of your evening left after finishing it. Plus, there are plenty more great books out there.

NOTE: Some people respond negatively to novel previewing because they like the surprise of what's coming up and do not want to have a peep at what's coming up. At the other extreme there are people who read the last few pages, find out how it all ends and then begin reading their novel! If they like the ending, they will read the whole book. If the ending perturbs them, they will move on to another book.

The choice is yours. I do recommend previewing at least the first three chapters of a book to make sure you are very familiar with the main characters and situations. This is especially useful with novels where there are loads of people, organizations, technology and places to remember. Without a firm foundation you may be quite lost later on. Just be aware of this: whenever you read without previewing, your comprehension and recall will be lower than if you did preview.

Previewing for readers of English as a second language

If your first language is not English, previewing may be even more important for you. There is really nothing that increases comprehension like previewing.

Vocabulary

If your second language is English, it may mean that you have a challenge with vocabulary. If you feel you run into a lot of words you don't know, I have some advice for you. Identify those words when you preview. Look at the words around them (the sentence they are in) and try to get the meaning from the context. In plain language, see if the words they are surrounded by give you the likely meaning. If you can't get the meaning, then you have a few choices:

1   You can hope that it will make more sense when you go back and read all of the text. This would give you more context.

2   You can look up the word right away and learn the meaning. This interruption is better during previewing than during reading. This is probably the safest choice, especially if you add the word to your vocabulary list.

3   Determine that the word is not that important; that you do not need to know its meaning. This is the most dangerous choice, as you may guess wrongly.

If English is not your first language (or whatever other language you are now reading in), this is of more importance. You may have more vocabulary words to learn than the average native English reader. Your understanding of a word is less likely to be the correct meaning.

There are also many slang usages that may not be obvious. Although it takes longer, looking up words you are unsure of will help your understanding of the text. If you think of it as a learning experience it will be easier to do. Being certain of meaning may save you from embarrassment later on. Keep a list of these words and review them periodically. Monthly would be very good. See the section on learning vocabulary on page 241.

Questions to ask that will help with previewing

Magnetic questions

Magnetic questions will really help with your previewing before reading as well as when using a technique called parroting (you will see more about this in chapter 9). These are basic questions that apply to most material, whether written or spoken. When you can answer these six questions you understand the material. The questions are:

Who?

What?

When?

Where?

Why?

How?

These simple questions cover the basic structure of information. These are the same questions asked by Rudyard Kipling in this extract from his poem *The Elephant's Child:*

> I keep six honest serving men
> (They taught me all I knew);
> Their names are What and Why and When
> And How and Where and Who.

Although we use them in a slightly different order, they are the same six questions and will serve us well too.

Who refers to people, organizations, characters, animals; whoever the subject of your reading material might be. For example, in an article about astronomy, the **Who** could be Galileo, Einstein, the Planetary Society or "people who believe the earth is flat."

What refers to the thing done (by a character) or a physical object in your reading material. Examples could be the first telescope, the Theory of Relativity, a black hole or the belief that the earth is at the center of the universe.

When refers to time. Examples could be important dates, seasons, eras or simply an indication of before or after. For example, "a long time ago," "during the Bronze Age," "20 July 1969," or "when he was a little boy."

Where refers to location. These are physical places such as countries, cities, a room in a house, under her left eye, behind the door or page 277 in a book.

Why refers to the reasons for something happening (cause and effect). This magnetic question takes us deeper into the meaning of what we're reading. Examples might be "because he felt driven to find the answer," or "because it was important to know when crops should be planted," or "because he knew how to ask the right questions." **Why** questions are usually the hardest to answer because we must have a fairly deep understanding of the material. Discovering "why" can give us a logical understanding of the world.

These first four questions are "factual" in nature. They give us the bare facts. **Why** begs us to look beyond the facts into motivations or cause and effect. People who can answer **Why** questions show true understanding of what they have read. This is what *you* are aiming for. You want to go beyond simple factual recall into true understanding.

How refers to methods of getting things done, whether by humans, nature or whatever. For example, "by working day and night for two weeks," or "by fastening part A securely to part C," or "by pure chance," or "because she would not give up until the company agreed." **How** questions are the nuts and bolts of the action in a story. They give us understanding of the methods used to achieve something or the mechanics of something happening. **How** can also quantify units of time, quantity and detail. **How** many people attended the meeting? **How** does this machine work better than the old model? **How** will you know when the project is finished?

To use the magnetic questions for previewing, write them on a card (used as a bookmark) near what you are reading. Glance at it before you start reading to remind your brain to be on the lookout for answers to these questions. While it's in your peripheral vision, your subconscious will be aware of it. Soon it will become second nature to be able to answer the magnetic questions after reading. For most of what you read, if you can answer those questions, you've got it! They are called "magnetic" because they begin to draw the important information to you like a magnet! You can also use the magnetic questions for parroting (chapter 9) and reviewing (chapter 10).

ASSIGNMENT

For at least 21 days, carry a magnetic questions bookmark with you and leave it by the side of your reading. Glance at it for five seconds before you start reading. Notice how certain words are jumping out at you.

Title questions

Most people pay very little attention to the titles of what they are reading. In fact, they tend to just skip straight past them. I've got people to read an article and then asked them what the title was. In a sample of several thousand people, about a dozen knew the title. That's a pretty strong statistic for people attending a reading course. You might think they would really be on their toes and try their best. Well, at the beginning, maybe that is their best!

How to do title questions

Read the title of the book, chapter or story. Ask yourself magnetic questions about the title and mentally fill in your answers as you read.

For example, a book is entitled *The Four Entertainers*:

Who are these four entertainers?

What do they do as the four entertainers?

When did they become the four entertainers?

Where are the four entertainers working?

Why are there the four entertainers?

How did they become the four entertainers?

HINT: When asking title questions be sure to repeat as much of the title in your question as possible. It may seem tedious or repetitious, but that's part of the point. There are two advantages to this. One is that by repeating the words in the title you have a much better chance of remembering the title. By asking these rapid-fire questions you are generating the curiosity to find the answers. Your questions may or may not make sense. It doesn't matter one bit. You are generating interest in the story. When you have finished reading the book or article you should be able to either answer the question or know with confidence that the question did not apply.

Many people try to make the title questions technique more complicated than it is. It is a very simple procedure. It should not take longer than about fifteen seconds. Go fast, have fun and do not be concerned about making sense. Just asking a few quick questions is all it takes. Keep it simple.

SUMMARY

- Previewing allows your mind to prepare for the task ahead and greases the wheels for brilliant reading.

- With the possible exception of reading poetry, previewing is one of the most powerful ways to increase your ability to read at speed, understand and recall any text that you've read.

- Previewing is always in the top three of the tools that SuperReading™ graduates say made the most difference to their reading.

- If English is your second language, do a lot of previewing. It saves time and you have a better understanding of the material when you are finished. You are also likely to remember more.

- You are free to combine any and all of the previewing techniques. This can be especially helpful on "bad days" when your cognitive abilities are not as efficient as usual.

8.

Eye-Hop™

My unique Eye-Hop™ exercises lie at the heart of learning how to become a super reader and they set SuperReading™ apart from any other type of speed reading. These exercises will lift you up to higher and higher reading speeds while maintaining your comprehension. When I am teaching I tell every class: "Whoever does the most Eye-Hop™ sessions will see the highest percentage increase in their reading effectiveness (R.E.) score." This almost always turns out to be true. Of course, you must also practice your reading each day!

We have already looked at the problems of reading one word at a time and pronouncing all the words in your head (see page 78). You are now at the point where you will begin to overcome that barrier to reading speed. Hopefully you have been reading along with your finger for a while now and it's beginning to feel more and more natural. I know this is a lifestyle change, but you will get used to it. Remember to reserve judgment (see the importance of this on page 44), but if you are already feeling good about hand pacing, that's great.

The next steps, which will take you anywhere from three to eight weeks to master, will work in tandem with your hand pacing skills and you will find that soon the two techniques will come together in a synergistic way.

The aim of the Eye-Hop™ exercises, examples of which are located at the end of this chapter on page 126, is to help you go from reading one word at a time to reading groups of words at a time, starting with groups of two words, moving on to three and four, to possibly five and six or more. You will learn, by repeating the exercises before going on to reading your own material, how to glance at a word group and understand its meaning at once. Once you start to do this you will save time but also you will reduce wear and tear on your eye muscles. The ocular muscles around the eye are among the weakest in the human body. When you read, the ocular muscles tend to refocus on every word. When you read four or five words at a time, they only need to focus a fraction as much. This will allow you to read longer with higher performance and less strain.

The concept of Eye-Hop™ has been around since about 1995. The first Eye-Hop™ was literally cut and pasted and then photocopied, and a typical article took three to four hours to produce. I created the Eye-Hop™ stories like this for several years.

Several Silicon Valley programmers who had taken

my course offered to write programs for me that would do it automatically, but with no success. Then in 2000, a student called Reto Stamm approached me as I was putting away my materials. He also offered to write a program to make Eye-Hop™. It took him a couple of hours and a little tweaking, before the Eye-Hop™ program ran perfectly. Now anyone can make their own Eye-Hop™ in seconds, thanks to the genius of Reto Stamm.

How to Eye-Hop™

The progression of Eye-Hop™ is to start reading two words at a time. When you have mastered that, then you move up to three words at a time, then four words, then five. When you get fast at reading four words, you will notice that your brain is no longer pronouncing many of the words inside your head. You are getting the full meaning of the phrase without pronouncing it! This is known as "the breakthrough." If this doesn't happen for you with four words, it will certainly happen with the five-word Eye-Hop™. There is little chance of reading five words in half a second and pronouncing them all.

Before moving on to the basics of Eye-Hop™ you should turn to page 126, where you will find examples of the exercises. Take a very quick look at them now so that you understand what the two-word Eye-Hop™ looks like. Once you are ready to start work on the

Eye-Hop™ exercises, you will need to go to my website (www.superreading.com/eyehop) where you will find all the exercises you need, arranged in booklets. You will probably need to print out the four Eye-Hop™ booklets, as I know that working from printed copies works very well. You may be able to do Eye-Hop™ exercises on a laptop, but be very careful not to stress your arm and shoulder. Most people like to touch when they read and hop, so you need to decide whether you want to be touching your computer screen that often. Having said that, tablet PCs are great for reading so perhaps consider one for your next computer purchase.

Each Eye-Hop™ booklet is a PDF file. The four booklets average about 50 single-sided pages each, totaling just over 200 printed pages. You may print them out as you need them, or all at once. Most people report they can print out the entire set of four booklets on one black ink cartridge with an inkjet printer. There are only graphics on the instruction page, which are not heavily ink intensive, and print well on your printer's text setting. The booklets print in "landscape mode," though your printer might work that out for itself. Although the pages are numbered, I recommend stapling them. Either take them to a copy shop with a heavy duty stapler, or separate a booklet in half or thirds to at least keep part of it together. You do not want to have the pages loose, as it would be difficult to pick them all up if a booklet blew out of your hands on a windy day!

These are the basics of Eye-Hop™:

- Either lay the Eye-Hop™ exercises flat in front of you when you practice, or up at a slight angle if that suits you better.

- To Eye-Hop™ you pivot from your elbow and actually HOP with your index finger from word group to word group (some people do use other fingers such as the middle one, or all four fingers, but this is quite rare). When hopping, your hand actually **comes off the paper or the screen**. Your fingertip traces a little half-circle from group to group. When you land, aim for the middle of each word group. See the Eye-Hop™ diagram below or in your printed Eye-Hop™ booklet. It summarizes all you need to know.

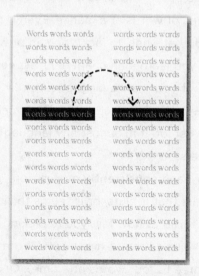

Use your finger to hop from column to column while doing the Eye-Hop™ exercises

- Slide the page up with your left hand as you go. (Left-handers reverse instructions as required.)

- Remember to go as fast as you can **while maintaining comprehension**.

- You need to do at least five minutes of Eye-Hop™ at a sitting (but not more than ten minutes, the first time—see below). It takes a few minutes to get into a rhythm. My suggestion is to read the Eye-Hop™ exercises at least three times per day for five to ten minutes per session. Try to manage at least 30 minutes of Eye-Hop™ per day. Forty minutes per day is ideal. Once you get used to it, there is no upper limit.

- Don't worry if you know the stories told in the exercises. It's actually OK to know these stories very well. The purpose of the exercises is to get you to understand groups of words at a glance. Even if they seem memorized, that's fine. In fact, you can preview these stories (as you learned in chapter 7), especially if English is not your native language. And if you make your own Eye-Hop™, which you will learn about below, you can do it in almost any language that uses Arabic letters.

- When your hand **consistently** moves from group to group so fast that it blurs, or it seems to slow you down compared to how fast you're picking up the words, move up to the next level (i.e., from two to three, or three to four words at a time). Once you move up a level, do not move back to the previous

level, even if you find you slow down in the new level,
which does happen (especially moving from three-
word to four-word Eye-Hop™).

- Finally, when you do the Eye-Hop™, stay relaxed.
  Keep your muscles loose. This is also true whenever
  you read. Staying relaxed is good advice for most
  activities.

WARNING! Reading for more than ten minutes with Eye-
Hop™ is not recommended **the first time you try it**. There
have been a handful of people over the years that got a
headache from doing this. It's very rare, and it only
happened to each of them once. I want to protect you.

NOTE: For now, the only time you hop is when you are
actually doing the Eye-Hop™ exercises. You don't hop
yet when reading text. Keep on using hand pacing for
regular reading. Later you will merge your Eye-Hop™
skills with the hand pacing, but only when you are ready.
I will explain more about that later. Once you're into
the four-word Eye-Hop™ you can start to use it on regular text.

Making your own Eye-Hop™

One of the best pieces of news I have for you is that
you can also produce your own personalized Eye-
Hop™. You can do this quickly and easily by going

online (www.superreading.com/hopify) and dropping any text in and clicking the "Hopify" button. Here are the steps for creating your own Eye-Hop™:

- Locate the text you want to Hopify
- Highlight that text
- Copy text
- Open the website (www.superreading.com/hopify)
- Click once in the big box
- Paste text
- Choose the level of Eye-Hop™ you require
- Choose your spacing
- Click the Hopify button.

At this point you have two choices. You can print out from the screen, or you can export the hopified text to a program like MS Word. Then you can print it out from there.

Eventually your best choice will be to do the Eye-Hop™ directly on your computer screen using a tablet PC.

NOTE: When creating your own Eye-Hop™, start off with relatively simple material. This is especially true when doing the two-word and three-word Eye-Hop™. Really dense or technical material makes learning the skill more difficult. Once you have developed your competence, you can begin to use more difficult material. This is why the prepared materials you download begin with such simple stories as Aladdin. In the beginning it's more important to develop your skill than to try to absorb highly technical subjects. You can move on to those later on. In conclusion, keep your hopping materials simple and easy to absorb.

ASSIGNMENT

You can make your own Eye-Hop™ any time you like. Start off with the prepared two-word Eye-Hop™ booklet to make sure you have a good sample to begin with. Once you know how doing Eye-Hop™ feels, then you may create your own. You will probably be able to do this within an hour of using the prepared Eye-Hop™.

Moving through successive levels

The beauty of Eye-Hop™ is that you expand your ability to absorb groups of words in easy to handle stages. On the following pages are examples of Eye-Hop™ stories and articles, which will give you the idea of how it works. Start by doing the two-word Eye-Hop™ at a pace that allows you to understand what you are reading. As always, go as fast as you can while maintaining comprehension. Once you have the feel for it after a couple of minutes, go at the same pace (or a bit faster) on the five-word Eye-Hop™. You will soon see that you cannot handle it if you do a hop about every second or so. It's simply too much information to grab all at once. The good news is that over the next few weeks you will be able to move up to that skill level and you will be able to handle it. If you try it now and cannot do it, you will better appreciate how far you will have come later. Some day you may read these words again and marvel at how you were able to increase your abilities.

Your next question might be, "When do I move up from two-word to three-word Eye-Hop™?" Although this information was given a couple of paragraphs back, I know that your reading skills aren't "super" yet, so I'm repeating it now! The simple answer is, when your finger is bouncing so fast from group to group that it becomes a blur, it's time to move up to the next higher word group. While you may find the two-word Eye-Hop™ less than challenging, I would like you to read through it completely at least once. Everyone is different. You may have to spend a week or more on the two-word. That's OK. Some people can actually start on the three-word Eye-Hop™ straight away, but I still get them to go through the two-word Eye-Hop™ at least once. There are important concepts to grasp in there.

It's very important not to move to the next level before you are ready. Make sure you are really blazing through before going on to the next higher word group. Likewise, don't stay too long on the two- or three-word Eye-Hop™. For example, it should not take you more than a week on the three-word Eye-Hop™, unless you found the two-word very challenging. It's probably better to err on the side of taking an extra hour or two before moving up.

Now, start reading at the beginning of the two-word Eye-Hop™ exercises. When you have read for between five and ten minutes, stop and begin again later from where you left off. Keep cycling through the stories until you are ready to move up to the next level. You may find yourself nearly memorizing the stories. That's fine. The major purpose of Eye-Hop™ is to get your brain to recognize groups of words at a glance. The more you become convinced of your ability, the better you will do.

If you like you can preview a couple of lines per page to familiarize yourself the first time you go through a story. This may be particularly helpful if English is not your first language. And remember, the same rule applies in Eye-Hop™ as in hand pacing: hop as fast as you can while maintaining comprehension.

NOTE: If your first language is not English, previewing the Eye-Hop™ may help you a lot. This was not something I anticipated when I was developing SuperReading™, but I noticed that students with English as a second language struggled a bit more with Eye-Hop™ than others. They hand paced more slowly, and their comprehension was lower. I found that previewing helped them to improve comprehension and see an increase in speed. If English is not your first language you will need to be a bit more patient with Eye-Hop™, particularly at four and five words, but you may find previewing will improve your ability.

Eye-Hop™ samples

Two-Word Eye-Hop™

Basic Astronomy

A few	thousand years
ago, Man	did not
even know	whether the
Earth was	round or
flat. A	few hundred
years ago,	he knew it
was round,	but did
not know	whether it
was the	center of
the universe,	or just
one of	the many
planets orbiting	the Sun.
Today he	is beginning
to wonder	whether there
is life	elsewhere in
the universe.	And, if
there are	intelligent beings,
how can	we get
in touch	with them.
For several	thousand years
Man has	wondered about
the nature	and behavior
of all things	to be
seen in	the sky.
He has	learned a

great deal

by watching

the Sun,

the Moon,

planets, meteors,

comets and

the other

heavenly bodies.

Our Sun

is a star.

The bodies

orbiting a star

are known

as planets.

Those orbiting

planets are

known as moons.

Astronomy is

the study of

all these

heavenly bodies.

Some people

may think

it strange

that a

science that

began several

thousand years

ago cannot

yet answer

the question:

"Is there

life elsewhere."

But when

we consider

the huge

distances and

time involved,

it's amazing

that we

know as

much as

we do.

We know

that our

Solar System

was born

at least

five thousand

million years ago.

Three-Word Eye-Hop™

Journey to the South Pole

The history of our involvement at
the South Pole dates back to the
early years of the 20th century.
It is a story of great explorers,
such as Scott, Amundsen, Shackleton
and Byrd. It is a story which
demonstrates the incredible advances
in technology which have taken place
during the last century. It all stems
from our natural curiosity and our
desire to know all we can
about our world. Robert Falcon Scott
of Great Britain led the first
major expedition to Antarctica in 1901.
He built a hut on Ross Island
and from there did scientific and
exploratory work. Scott, along with
Dr. Edward Wilson and Ernest Shackleton
(later Sir Ernest) made the first
journey to the interior of the
frozen continent. They walked 200
miles south on the Ross Ice Shelf.
It is doubtful whether they believed
they had much chance of reaching
the South Pole, but their march
was the first in that direction.
Their decision to turn back was

made in part
illness, which was
to scurvy (a
Following his return
became determined to
to lead his
1907 he returned
in charge of
greatest expeditions
His men became
climb Mt. Erebus
on Ross Island.
the south magnetic
importantly they pioneered
the South Pole.
Jameson Adams
with four ponies,
the pole in
Dogsleds were
of 1901 to 1904
not work out
For this reason,
to rely on
The journey south
The ponies pulled
The explorers traveled
shelf, wondering if
the South Pole.
and they had
just 97 miles

because of Shackleton's
felt to be due
deficiency of vitamin C).
to England, Shackleton
return to Antarctica
own expedition. In
to Ross Island
one of the
in Antarctic history.
the first to
the 13,000-foot volcano
They also discovered
pole, but most
the route to
Shackleton, Frank Wild,
and Eric Marshall,
set out for
October 1908.
used in the expedition
and they did
well at all.
Shackleton had decided
ponies and manpower.
was remarkable.
very large loads.
over the ice
it would lead to
It did not,
to turn back
from the Pole.

Four-Word Eye-Hop™

The Optimist

There is a story of identical twins.
One of them was a hope-filled optimist.
"Everything is coming up roses!" he would say.
The other was a sad and hopeless pessimist.
He thought that Murphy, as in Murphy's Law,
was an optimist. The worried parents of
the boys brought them to the local psychologist.
He suggested to the parents a plan to
balance the twins' personalities. "On their next birthday,
put them in separate rooms to open their gifts.
Give the pessimist the best toys you can afford,
and give the optimist a box of manure."
The parents followed these instructions and carefully
observed the results. When they peeked in
on the pessimist, they heard him audibly complaining,
"I don't like the color of this computer . . .
I'll bet this calculator will break . . .
I don't like this game . . . I know someone
who's got a bigger toy car than this . . ."
Tiptoeing across the corridor, the parents peeked in
and saw their little optimist gleefully throwing the manure
up in the air. "You can't fool me!
Where there's this much manure, there's
gotta be a pony!' *Author unknown*

Five-Word Eye-Hop™

A humble Scottish farmer

This story begins with a poor
trying to make a living for
for help coming from a nearby
and ran to the bog. There,
muck, was a terrified boy,
free himself. The farmer saved
been a slow and terrifying
carriage pulled up to the
An elegantly dressed nobleman
himself as the father of the
"I want to repay you," said
son." "No, I can't accept
Scottish farmer said, waving
the farmer's own son came
hovel. "Is that your son?"
the farmer replied proudly.
me take him and give him
is anything like his father,
can be proud of." And that
son graduated from St. Mary's
London, and went on to become
as the noted Sir Alexander
penicillin. Years afterward,
with pneumonia. What saved
of the nobleman? Lord Randolph
Sir Winston Churchill.
around comes around.

Scottish farmer. One day while
his family, he heard a cry
bog. He dropped his tools
mired to his waist in black
screaming and struggling to
the lad from what could have
death. The next day, a fancy
Scotsman's sparse surroundings.
stepped out and introduced
boy the farmer had saved.
the nobleman. "You saved my
payment for what I did," the
off the offer. At that moment,
to the door of the family
the nobleman asked. "Yes,"
"I'll make you a deal. Let
a good education. If the lad
he'll grow to be a man you
he did. In time, the farmer's
Hospital Medical School in
known throughout the world
Fleming, the man who discovered
the nobleman's son was stricken
him? Penicillin. The name
Churchill. His son's name?
Someone once said: What goes
It might be true.

Mastering Eye-Hop™

You will want to have fairly good comprehension while Eye-Hopping™. You can test your comprehension by parroting after a story (as you will learn in chapter 9). You should be able to remember at least 75 percent of the content—not word for word, but the gist of the story with some interesting details such as names and places. The rule is to read as fast as you can while maintaining comprehension. This is especially true if you have previewed the Eye-Hop™ story (see chapter 7). If you have done poorly, then slow down a bit on the next story and parrot again. If your recall is still too low, and you are not overly stressed or distracted by things in your life, then preview the stories. If that does not help, then do not worry. Just keep going through the Eye-Hop™ exercises as best you can and eventually they will do their work for you. Then you will start pattern reading (to find out all about this, see page 162) when you are into either the four-word or five-word Eye-Hop™.

ASSIGNMENT

Do at least 40 minutes of Eye-Hop™ every day until you have mastered the five-word level.

SUMMARY

- The purpose of Eye-Hop™ is to move you from processing one word at a time to many words at a time. You progress through the levels, getting faster and faster on each level until your finger cannot physically keep up with your brain.

- At the two-word and three-word levels you will still hear all the words in your head as you process them. When picking up speed in the four-word level you will begin to experience some drop-off of the words pronounced while still understanding the meaning of those words.

- You should have fairly good comprehension when Eye-Hopping™.

- You can parrot (see chapter 9) to see what you recall. If your recall is very low, you probably need to slow down.

- Sometimes you slow down for a while when moving up to a next level (particularly when going from three-word to four-word).

- Your finger should come off the page when you hop, defining each word group as you land.

- You can create your own Eye-Hop™ by copying text and importing it into the Hopify website (www.superreading.com/hopify).

9.

Parroting

Parroting is an extremely useful technique for testing yourself on what you have read. It has a key role to play in boosting comprehension and recall. You can parrot at various points in your reading: certainly, while you are learning the techniques of SuperReading™, you should parrot at least once a day, after reading key sentences (see page 93). The idea is that you read a few key sentences, and then you find out how much you remember. For example, if you were to read eight key sentences you may be able to recall points from only five of them. Some people can only remember two or three points. Wherever you start is OK. It's where you end up that is important! Of course, when you are parroting, you will find that how much you can recall will depend on how you are feeling that day. We have already looked at some of the factors that can affect our reading abilities, but it is worth recalling them now:

- adequate sleep
- nutrition
- interest in the material
- stress
- your environment (noise, physical distractions).

In this chapter we will also look at some useful techniques for dealing with test stress in the exam room.

> **ASSIGNMENT**
>
> Pick up any book with paragraphs. Read eight key sentences (see page 93) and discover how many you can recall. With eyes open or closed, recall everything you can about what you just read. You don't do it verbatim; instead you are simply "paraphrasing." This means that you are remembering the gist of the information.
>
> Do this assignment at least three times to make up a good sample. Now the idea is to build up your ability over time, once you have taken on board the information in the rest of this chapter. This technique is called "stair stepping" and is a very powerful way to build your skills. It allows you to know your level of skills when you begin, how fast you're making progress and where you end up.

How to parrot

There are three ways to parrot. Have a go at all of them and see which works best for you. Remember in chapter 3 you worked out what kind of learner you are? If you are a visual or kinesthetic type person you may find that the Info-Map™ technique (see pages 147–51) works particularly well for you. If you are more of an auditory person, you may find that verbal parroting works better. In either case you will want to practice both, as your skills will improve and your abilities will expand.

Parroting by writing

The first parroting method is to write down what you can remember. The best way to do this is by using the Info-Map™ technique for note taking. This is a great method for generating ideas, as you will see when you come to try it out. We will look at this technique again in much more detail in chapter 10, where it is used for reviewing what you have read, but to put it simply, Info-Mapping™ is a technique to map out information instead of writing it down in serial order. One advantage of Info-Mapping™ is that you may record information in any order you choose, either by category or the order in which you remember it. Information is bullet pointed (using key words) to remind you of the various points you have read.

The idea is that when you have finished previewing and then reading your pages, write down the central theme within the circle or oval drawn in the middle of your Info-Map™. Send several lines (usually five to seven) out from the central hub and write down the main thoughts.

From each one of these thoughts, extend a line or two. Write down other thoughts as you remember them. Try to group similar ideas together. Write as fast as you can without much regard to being neat.

When you are parroting by writing, you are either reading **or** writing. Do not look at the book, write, look at the book, and write. The best way is to read, put the book down, then create your Info-Map™ **from memory**.

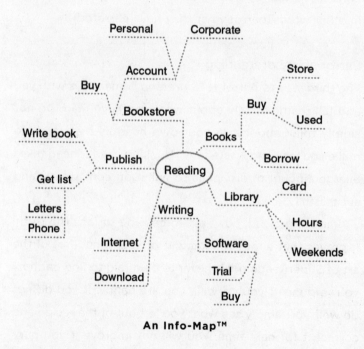

An Info-Map™

Parroting by telling
The second way to parrot is to tell what you remember to someone else. This makes absorbing the information

multisensory. You see it, you say it and you hear it. In class students always stand up when parroting with someone else. That gets you to think on your feet (which may also come in handy for other situations).

It's been said that the best way to learn something is to teach it to someone else. In essence, this is what you are doing when you **tell** the other person what you've read. If you parrot with another person, you can hone your listening skills further by writing down what they have told you. In other words, parrot what they have parroted!

Parroting by pretending

The third way to parrot is to *pretend* someone is with you and tell them verbally about what you have read. Do **not** simply think about it in your own head as that tends to make you lazy and waste time. Thinking in your head takes a large amount of discipline to pull it off consistently and successfully.

Parroting aloud, however, forces you to face the truth. It proves that either you know it or you don't. Part of the art of SuperReading™ is never to be afraid to find out how you've done. If you do well, you are happy. If you do not do well, you simply see what you left out of the recipe and correct it for next time. You will not improve if you bury your head in the sand as denial has no place in any plan to improve your skills. There is a phrase used in NLP (neuro-linguistic programming) which is especially apt: "There is no failure, only feedback."

While you are telling your pretend companion about what you have read, use the magnetic questions (who, what, when, where, why, how—see page 108). They make a great starting point for quizzing yourself on the material you have read. Simply ask yourself "Who was mentioned?," "What did they do?," "When did they do that?," "Where did they do that?" and so on.

ASSIGNMENT

Parrot for at least one five-minute piece of reading every day. This time use the Info-Map™ technique (pages 147–51).

Dealing with test stress

Some people get really stressed and flustered in testing situations such as exams. They feel like they know the information beforehand, but something awful happens when they walk through that doorway into the exam room. Their heart rate goes up, their palms get sweaty, their skin grows cold and sometimes their mouth goes dry. Their head may swim and their breathing goes shallow. These are all signs of panic. Are there solutions? Yes.

Using parroting techniques will get you testing yourself more thoroughly than your teacher, professor or anyone else. You will have much higher confidence, borne out of proving to yourself that you know the information. Memorizing through pictures and imagination (see pages 192 and 230) will take the stress away from trying to get facts and concepts to simply stick in your head. Affirmations and visualization will get you through the rough patches (see page 192).

You can also use a couple of physical methods to calm yourself down:

1   Make your breathing slow and deep for a couple of minutes. Only focus on your breathing—think of nothing other than the air entering and leaving your body. You can hold on to it for a few seconds when you fill your lungs.

2   The other technique is "palming." This will relax your eyes and your mind. Rub your hands together very fast with a good amount of pressure. When they heat up cup your eyes with them, letting the heel of your hand fit into your eye socket. Keep it there for five to ten seconds. This will relax the ocular muscles and give you a feeling of relaxation. It may take you a few seconds to get focused again! You will feel more calm and may even find yourself smiling.

You can also perform a minute of alphabet animals (see page 220).

Easy does it

Here's a specific strategy that works well for dealing with test stress. When you open your paper, preview the test (using the techniques in chapter 7), pick out all the easy items and do them first. This has three advantages. One is that you will definitely get credit for those questions. Another is that it will build your confidence. The third is that it will give you momentum to get going on the rest of the test.

SUMMARY

- Testing yourself is a great way to determine how much information you have gleaned from your reading.

- There are three ways to accomplish this: one is to write down what you remember; a second way is to tell someone else what you can recall; the third method is to pretend to tell someone else what you remember.

- Testing will ensure that you recall the information.

- If you only parrot in your head, you will tend to get lazy and not follow through. Saying the words out loud proves that you really do remember what you read.

- Use calming techniques in testing situations.

10.

Reviewing and embodying

Reviewing is a very useful technique that helps you to fill in the gaps and answer those questions that previewing and reading left behind. You use reviewing after you parrot what you've just read. As you review, you will need to keep the questions or gaps in your reading in mind and make mental notes when you discover the missing information. This is reading with a specific purpose and is known as targeted reading.

We will also look at Info-Mapping™ again in more detail in this chapter as it is a very valuable technique for aiding review and recall. Embodying is the act of putting information into long-term memory, or possibly medium-term memory. A difference is that repetition of the information over time (weeks to months) may be the factor that pushes medium-term memories into long-term ones. An embodied idea is one that requires very little thought to access and communicate. An example would be the answer to 6 × 6. It takes only a fraction of a second to say the answer, because that information has been embodied. It requires no great degree of intelligence or ability. The answer to 16 × 16 requires more thought and work. While the answer, 256, is something you know, it was probably not associated with the question of what is 16 × 16. You've heard tell of 256; you just didn't embody the fact that it is the product of 16 × 16. What you do have stored in long-term memory is the procedure for figuring it out, either on paper, in your head or with a calculator. In this chapter we will be looking at various methods for embodying information.

Simple reviewing techniques

Before going on to describe some helpful reviewing techniques I should tell you that if you have parroted (chapter 9) and you are already able to recall everything you need for that session, you may then skip reviewing. However, if you have previewed (chapter 7), read and parroted and realize you are missing something vital, then you need to go back and review the section containing the vital piece of information. Use the following simple techniques (which we have already covered in chapter 7 when you used them for previewing purposes) for better recall.

Key sentence
Read the key sentences (see page 93) of each paragraph again. They are most likely to be the first sen-

tence of each paragraph, but may be the last sentence. Look at how the author organizes the information and adapt to it.

Name and number scan

Scan the page for proper nouns and numbers to remind you of the facts in the text. Use your finger when you scan. Stop on each one for a second or two to let the information sink in. You can say the word(s) aloud for extra impact (see below for more on this).

Simple scanning

You can simply scan over material you just read to see if specific pieces of information, such as names, dates, places, etc., jump out at you. Remember to use your finger!

Further memory techniques for reviewing and recalling

There follows a range of techniques that you might find helpful when you are reviewing and recalling what you have read. Try all those that appeal to you and stick with the ones you like. While some techniques work better for some people than others, I would suggest trying each for at least 21 days or 21 times, and then judge which really works best for you.

- Use the Roman room memory technique (which you will find out more about on pages 233–9) to recall lists of items. Take each item to remember in turn and link it with the next object in the memory room.

- Use the short-term method of mental shouting, where you pretend you are in an expensive restaurant, standing on a table, shouting out the thing you need to remember as loud as you can. (There is more on this too, on page 230.)

- Emotion is another tool you can use to seal in information. Get excited about something and you're more likely to remember it. You can use joy or enthusiasm or countless other emotions. (Again, there is more on this, on page 229.)

- Strong imagery (see page 192) related to the topic will help a lot, as the right brain is activated by pictures.

- Acting the topic out in some way can be very powerful, as it gets the entire body into the performance. This can be very kinesthetic, verbal and emotional all in one.

- Sheer repetition is another way. Simply go over and over the information until it sticks.

The most powerful method of repetition is **"spaced repetition."** This is where you do some repetitions and then wait to repeat them again. You can wait anywhere from minutes to days, depending on how much information you are trying to absorb. For example, if you wanted to remember that the capital of Belgium is Brussels, or something more arcane, like the capital of Mongolia, which is Ulan Bator. If you were to look at that fact once a day for 21 days, you would probably remember it forever. So spend ten seconds on it one day and then another ten seconds the next day. Each time you do this you will experience the "Oh yeah phenomenon." When you ask yourself, "What is the capital of Mongolia?" you may not remember at first. When you look at the answer, you'll get a rush of recall, and say, "Oh yeah—it's Ulan Bator!" A couple of days later when you do it again, you may experience the same thing. Then you repeat this a week later and then a month later and so on each month. This will only have taken you five minutes, but spread out for 15 or 20 seconds at a time, it will have a huge effect on your remembering the answer. That little rush of recall really does something amazing in your brain and puts the information in your long-term memory almost effortlessly. All you have to do is choose the appropriate spacing to facilitate the remembering. The simpler and more familiar the information is the less spaced repetition you will need. For example, knowing that the Nile is the longest river in the world is relatively easy, because you've heard of the Nile, seen pictures of it, and can imagine it on a map. However, remembering that the Ob-Irtysh is the fifth longest river requires far more repetition because for most people they have never heard of it and probably have no idea where it is (Russia). Remembering the Nile as the longest river could probably be embodied in five seconds once a day for a week. Remembering the Ob-Irtysh as the fifth longest river could take 15 seconds once a day for a week, then once a week for six weeks, and once a month for four months. There's no hard and fast rule, but I would say, with the Ob-Irtysh example, if you had it well recalled after three months, I would do a couple of extra months just in case. The great thing about this method is that it takes so little time. Everyone can spare a few seconds in a day. You could even program the information to pop up on your computer or mobile device on a regular basis until it is embodied.

Note taking by Info-Mapping™

As we have already seen in chapter 9, Info-Mapping™ is a form of laying out information in a graphic form instead of in a linear fashion like most people are taught in school. Instead of Roman numeral I, I (a), I (b), I (c), II, II (a), II (b), etc., the Info-Map™ spreads out in a radial fashion from the central hub. This style gives the note taker the freedom to place information wherever it seems to fit, and even if it does not fit well it doesn't matter that much. In practice, Info-Mapping™ is less stressful than a list because you do not have to remember information in the exact same order as the author. When trying to recall information (by parroting, see chapter 9), we sometimes feel that if there is a gap, we cannot proceed until we recall that fact. We feel stuck, frustrated and stupid. With Info-Mapping™ you can simply move on to another area and write down what you recall from there. As there is no sequence required, you are free to move in any direction.

You can use Info-Mapping™ to help you review and recall. When you have finished previewing and reading your material, write down the central theme in the circle or oval in the middle of your Info-Map™. Send several lines (usually five to seven) out from the central hub and write down the main thoughts at the ends of the lines. From **each one** of those thoughts extend as many lines as you need outward from that thought or fact. Write down other thoughts as you remember them. Try to group similar ideas together. Write as fast as you can without much regard to being neat.

Only use one circle or oval for the middle of your Info-Map™. This way, if you write something important, you can circle it later to draw attention to it. Six months later you will be able to look back at your Info-Map™ and instantly go to the most important points. Some Info-Mapping™ systems have you use color to distinguish various categories of information from one another. Colors are great if you have the time and always have colors with you. If you don't, you've become dependent on a system that has a small drawback. If you want a way to distinguish categories, you can use shapes. You can use circles, squares, squiggly lines, zigzag lines, loopy lines, double lines, etc. As long as you have a pen or pencil you're in business.

Then:

- review the pages you have just read
- fill in the knowledge gaps in your Info-Mapped™ notes after you review
- review the material again to fill in any remaining gaps.

When you are reviewing using your Info-Map™, you are either reading or writing. Do not look at the book, write, look at the book, and write. The best way is to read, put the book down, then Info-Map™ from memory. (By the way, forget using a highlighter pen—this just trains your brain to be lazy.)

When you write, you can either write on the line or at the end of the line. The choice is yours. Below are two examples to show the difference. You could combine the two methods and save a bit of room. Topics can go on the line and notes can go after the line. Whatever you are comfortable with is what will work best for you. The idea is to end up with a map that resembles the way you put information together. That way, when you look back on it in the future it will still make sense to you. You have organized it in a similar fashion as to how your brain processes and stores information.

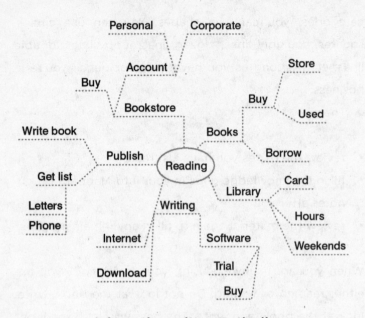

Information written on the line

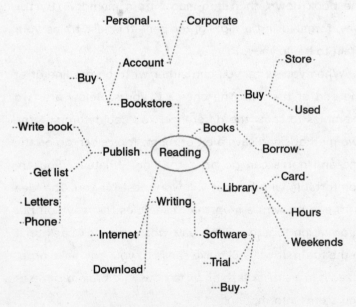

Information written after the line

In my classes I am always fascinated to see how, with the same instructions, everyone comes up with a totally different-looking map. Some are very neat and organized, some are helter-skelter, some are crowded and some look sparse. Each Info-Map™ reflects something of the personality of its creator. Whenever you create something it can't help but relate to who you are.

Advanced review techniques

Once your reading skills reach a certain level, you will be able to absorb and embody large amounts of information in a relatively short time. As you gently push yourself to do more and more each week, some amazing things will begin to happen. Eventually you will be able to read not only entire lines at a glance, but multiple lines. Some people, after a few months, are able to see and understand small paragraphs in a second or two. When this happens, it is important to just let the process take over. This is called relaxed focus, or directed relaxed focus.

You may feel like an observer watching the reading process as you read. This is a very right-brain activity. It must come with no analyzing and no judgment (whether good or bad). The first way to experience this is by reviewing some information in a loop several times or more. This is not the same as when people don't understand something and have to go back over it several times for it to make sense. You already under-stand it. Now you are working to permanently retain it. When you have retained it, you can say that you have embodied it. To embody the information you read means to make it a part of you; almost on a physical level.

For example, if you were to pattern read (see chapter 11) this page over and over 10 or 20 times, going faster and faster, eventually the information would be going directly into your subconscious mind. You would find that you could bring up any part of it with ease and confidence. This method of combining repetition and pattern reading puts you in the zone far beyond what any standard reader could hope for.

Advanced Eye-Hop™

Simply hop down the page when you are reviewing, skip-ping several lines as you go. This works especially well when you're very fast at four-word Eye-Hop™, as your brain is picking up more content. A variation on this theme is the "roving Xs." Trace three big letter Xs down the page (see the diagram opposite) and then parrot. Use this pattern to review extra-wide columns because pattern reading is more difficult with really wide columns (see chapter 11 for a detailed explanation of pattern reading). You may have to do three hops to a line in some books and articles with very wide columns.

Roving Xs

Loop the loop

With this technique you simply make a looping pattern (see diagram on the next page) with your finger on the first page and repeat it on the facing page. Keep going for as many pages as you wish to review (you can also use this for previewing). Consciously you may not remember tremendous amounts. Subconsciously, your mind remembers everything. You may do one large loop on a page, or two or three smaller loops. The diagram shows one large loop per page. You can experiment with other patterns as well. You could try a pattern like a lightning bolt, or a figure eight. Sometimes being creative with a pattern gets you more interested in the text.

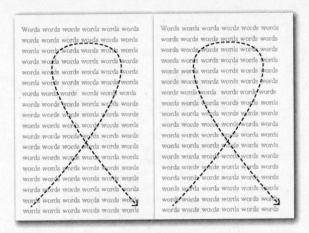

Loop the loop

Page scan

With this reviewing technique, you start at the bottom of a page and let your eyes move up the page like a scanning device. When you get to the top, let your eyes scan back down the same way. Again, this technique is most powerful when you've been going quite fast for a while with the four-word or five-word Eye-Hops™ (see chapter 8).

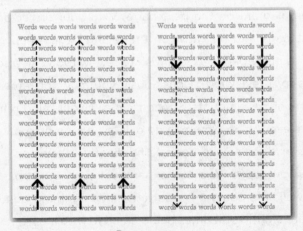

Page scan

Hop-drop

Hop-drop is a slightly different way of doing Eye-Hop™. Some people really like it. Others do not. Please try it while reserving judgment for at least 21 days. You lift your finger off the page and drop down a couple of lines, picking up the ones you go over as you proceed. You must be going quite fast on four-word Eye-Hop™ or fairly fast on the five-word for this technique to work. The narrower the column, the better it works.

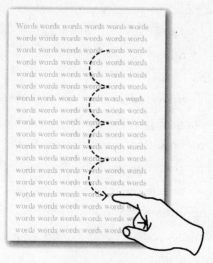

Hop-drop

NOTE: These are advanced techniques. You must be an advanced reader to take them on—in other words, you should have progressed to the five-word Eye-Hop™ before you can benefit from them. Often they do not work well the first time you use them and this is another instance where reserving judgment is crucial.

Also be aware that on a particular day you may or may not be at your mental best. This is a good reason to reserve judgment for at least 21 days! That way you are sure to catch yourself on a good day and reap the benefits of a particular skill.

It seems that on different days different techniques work better. This may be due to various cycles in our day, month or season. The reason doesn't really matter. What's important is to recognize that we are sometimes different and we need to have a varied set of tools to deal with these differences. For instance, if key sentencing just isn't working for you today, switch to name and number scan.

If variety is the spice of life, then experimenting is the spice of reading. Switching things around may wake up your brain, forcing it to focus better. Avoid getting into mental ruts by changing your thinking and actions.

If you keep on seeing yourself as the reader you want to be, the appropriate tool will work for you. The key is to keep believing in yourself and seeing yourself using the information you absorb.

Hi-speed review

By reviewing significant chapters, or even entire books, the subconscious accepts the information in a subliminal fashion, because the speeds are so high that you are not consciously aware of every word. What you do is simply keep reading in your favorite pattern faster and faster and faster. Soon the concepts are coming together in pictures in your mind like a movie.

ASSIGNMENT

Take a particularly significant piece of information and read it at high speeds until it becomes imagery. This will take several times of reading through; the number of times varying from person to person and day to day. It may take five, ten or twenty loops. Eventually you will register the meaning pictorially wherever possible, seeing the information more than just understanding it. This effect depends a bit on the nature of the subject. Anything in the text you can picture will become more vivid with each repetition. You are looking to turn it more into an experience than just reading it. You are mentally running it over and over like an endless loop tape. Allow it to seep deeply into your subconscious. Like doing repetitions in weight-lifting, the information will build up in that part of your personality. The high-speed loop is a wonderfully simple concept which cannot be achieved as well by standard readers. Your ability to absorb multiple words at a glance enables you to benefit from high-speed review at a much more significant level.

Daily application

Always look out for ways to practice a concept on a daily basis. For instance, you might pick a self-improvement book like *How to Win Friends and Influence People* by Dale Carnegie. One of his concepts is "You catch more flies with honey than with vinegar." In sales, or any human relations, we see that being "sweet" (nice) toward people takes you further than being a grouch or a critic. Focus on "using honey" all day long. Opportunities will present themselves. You could even focus on one attribute for a week. Benjamin Franklin identified several areas in which he wished to improve himself. One was humility. He carried around a card with the word "humility" written on it everywhere he went for a month. He claimed this helped him to be more humble. According to Franklin, "Humility is the one thing that once you think you have it—you don't!"

Look for clever ways to remind yourself daily of how you might wish to change. Be creative. Whatever works for you is what's right. The same principle applies to reviewing information. If you review information daily until it is embodied, you will soon find it difficult to forget. The difference between "review" and "application" is that with application you are putting the information to use, which better seals it into memory. If information you wish to remember does not have a way to be applied, you can imagine teaching it to someone else. In that case, teaching is the application.

Keep a notebook

For permanent long-term recall, I recommend keeping a notebook (or file) that can hold the information you are interested in always having at your "mental fingertips." Keep key words and concepts in it and review it monthly. It will only take a few minutes and you will remember all these wonderful concepts. Some can be factual; some can be inspirational; and others can be instructional. A quick perusal will be all you need to remind you and further embody the concepts in your mind. Put a monthly reminder in your calendar to review this file. It is the essence of spaced repetition (see page 145) and the ultimate expression of reserving judgment.

SUMMARY

- Repetition is one of the most powerful ways to embody information. The more exposures spread over time (spaced repetition), the more likely you are to remember.

- Using techniques such as Hi-speed review, advanced patterns of Eye-Hop™, Loop the Loop, Roving Xs and Page Scan can work at a non-verbal level to help you retain information.

- Info-Mapping™ is not only multimodal, it is a permanent record of what you wish to recall.

In this chapter we have looked at reviewing and embodying what you have read, and we have now come to the end of the section of this book that has introduced you to the basic techniques of SuperReading™. Now would be a good time to recap on what you should have learned so far. It is conveniently encapsulated in the acronym PREPARE:

Preview
REad
PArrot
Review
Embody

Put the underlined letters together and you have: P.RE.PA.R.E:

The first step is to **preview** the material so you know what's coming.

The second step is to **read** (using your finger, of course!).

Step three is a choice: **parroting** to see if you've gained enough information.

Step four is another choice based on what you learned in step three. If you are missing vital information, you then **review** to capture it.

Step five, **embodying**, is yet another choice: do I want to put effort into storing this information in medium- or long-term memory?

PART THREE:

Building on the Basics

11.

Pattern reading

By now you must have realized that there are many aspects of the art of reading, and in this chapter we are going on to look at some more advanced techniques that will help you to build on the basics of SuperReading™, including perhaps the most important concept in this book—pattern reading.

REMINDER: To remind yourself of the basics you have already learned, use your hand pacing technique (see chapter 6) to read something you have just previewed. (In fact, are you reading these words using your finger right now?) When you read, read every word including the key sentences again (or you can use name and number scan or novel previewing—see chapter 7). This repetition will aid your recall later. And remember, always read as fast as you can while maintaining comprehension. Think about increasing your speed about 5 percent or so per page. It's human nature to slow down, but most of the time there is no real need to do this—it just tends to happen. If you concentrate you will find you can speed up 5 percent with no loss to your comprehension. In fact, after a few weeks of practice, speeding up will probably increase your comprehension and recall.

Gentle snap-back or carriage return

This is a simple technique that will help you to improve your hand pacing.

When you get to the end of a line that you are hand pacing, "snap" your finger back to the left of the line of text (rather like the carriage return on an old manual typewriter). The snapping back is **not** a violent move. It is a firm, yet gentle snap. The intention of the action is to keep you moving and in flow with the text. It will help to challenge your brain to keep up.

When you get near the end of the line you may notice that you understand the whole line **before** your finger arrives at the last letter of the last word. As soon as you **know** the meaning of that line, snap down to the next line and do the same thing again.

Reading styles

You start reading after you have previewed a chapter, story or article that is greater than two paragraphs. For now, you will use **one** of the following techniques as you read. The first two, hand pacing and Eye-Hop™, are fundamental techniques, while the rest are more advanced. When you get to pattern reading on page 172 you will discover a technique that is the most important aspect of SuperReadingTM, and which will really help you to fulfill your potential.

Hand pacing

This is a brief reminder of the technique, which was explained in detail in chapter 6. Sitting in the proper reading position (see pages 73–4), elbow on the table, you pivot your arm so your finger moves in a smooth, flowing motion across the page. The finger always remains in motion, although you may slow down or speed up, depending on the material.

Eye-Hop™

Again, this is a brief reminder of the technique that was described in detail in chapter 8. You can read with this method by making two or three hops with your eyes across a line, dropping down to the next line and continuing in the same manner. If you are reading a book with exceptionally long lines of small type, you may have to do more than three bounces in the beginning. As always, you are going as fast as possible, or taking in as much as possible while maintaining your comprehension.

Second word

After you've mastered the two-word Eye-Hop™, you can really begin to benefit from the hard work you've done. You are now able to process two to three words at a glance, especially if the words are relatively small. Now, to take further advantage of your growing skill, you can start your finger on the second word of a line instead of the first. Your brain will process both the first word and the second word (and possibly the third word). This will begin to save you even more time because you will get down the page a bit faster. This is because even though you are reading at the same speed, you are covering a slightly smaller area, so it will take you less time to cover each line.

ASSIGNMENT

Pick up a book and try reading a paragraph or two now, starting on the second word, and you'll experience this for yourself. After reading a couple of paragraphs, parrot (see chapter 9) to see how that worked for you. Your recall should be the same (or better) as when you start with your finger at the very beginning of a line. If it is not, it may be that you are thinking about the technique instead of what you are reading, thus taking up some of your attention and focus. Assuming you have been doing the Eye-Hop™ exercises in chapter 8, this technique **will** work for you.

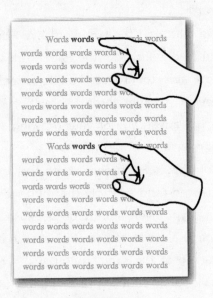

Second word

Short stroke

Once you have been reading fairly fast (about one line, or two hops per second or faster) in three-word Eye-Hop™ and are moving on to four-word Eye-Hop™ it's time for your next step—short stroke, which is an advanced form of hand pacing. Instead of starting with your finger at the first letter of each line and following through to the last letter of each line, you start in half an inch to an inch from the begin-ning and finish half an inch from the end. You will find that you can do this easily because you have been practicing the Eye-Hop™ exercises. You are now taking in and compre-hending at least three words at a time, probably four. If you start a line with your finger on the first letter, you are cutting off the two words that could be to the left of that point. So start further in to take advantage of your new ability.

The same holds true for the end of a sentence. Once you get near the end, you will find that you already know what it says.

Word darts

Word darts

To prepare for short stroke, you first need to have a look at the concept of "word darts," which is related to Eye-Hop™.

> **ASSIGNMENT**
>
> Find a book with reasonable-sized type (at least 11 or
>
> 12 pt or 16 character spaces (or less) per inch).

Now, with the book open to pages with plenty of text, choose some random lines and place your finger near the middle of the line as if you were doing Eye-Hop™. Your finger will only remain there for a moment, just like when doing Eye-Hop™. However, instead of going left-right-left-right, move down the page to "random" lines and just see what you get. In other words, you may hit the third line, the seventh line, the tenth, the fifteenth, the eighteenth and the twenty-fourth. Do at least a dozen of these word darts to get a good sample over a couple of pages. Afterward, you should know approximately how many words you were picking up with each "dart." Most people will pick up three. Some may pick up three or four, and a few will pick up four or five. If English is not your first language, you may only pick up two. If you want to feel better, try the same exercise in your native language.

Starting short stroke

Once you have determined how many words you pick up using word darts, the concept of short stroke will make more sense to you. In fact, short stroke is very easy. Simply place your finger down about an inch or so into the text as you begin a new line and start reading from there. Likewise, as you approach the end of that line, you will notice that you understand all the meaning of that line before your finger reaches the end! Once you know what the line means, drop down to the next line and "short stroke" that one about an inch. Keep going the same way to the bottom of the page as illustrated in the diagram.

Your brain has been getting used to picking up at least three words at a glance. This means that whenever you put your finger down on a page, your brain will pick up one to two words around it. Therefore, starting a line by putting your finger down on the first letter of the first word has your brain looking at the margin to the left for information. You can now put your finger down on the second word in the line and still have picked up the first word!

Short stroke

ASSIGNMENT

Begin with your finger near the solid line as shown in the diagram (about an inch in). When you get to about where the dashed line is you will already understand the remainder of the line. When that happens for you, drop down to the next line and begin again.

Short stroke will increase your comprehension after just a page or two of practice and will cut at least 20 percent off your reading time. Later, when you are going fast (about ten lines, or 20 hops, in eight seconds) on the four-word Eye-Hop™, you can start even further in. Try different starting points until you find what's comfortable for you. Once you know that, you can stretch yourself each day to increase your abilities. For example, once you've mastered starting in at 1 inch, try 1.5 inches. The same goes for ending your reading on a line. Keep ending further and further from the end of the line. Once that is consistently comfortable try starting in at 2 inches. Eventually, your entire stroke on a line will only be about 1 to 2 inches, situated in the middle of the page.

Evolution of short stroke

As you are able to absorb more and more words, your finger stroke across the page will get smaller and smaller. By the time you are picking up three to four words at a glance, you will be able to shorten your stroke to the size of the line marked 2 (see page 171). When you can pick up four or five words at a glance, your stroke will look like line 4. Eventually your stroke will be very short like lines 6 or 7. However, by that time you will probably be performing pattern reading (for more, see page 172 of this chapter). Sometimes you may still decide to use short stroke instead of pattern reading for various reasons, such as lack of sleep or stress.

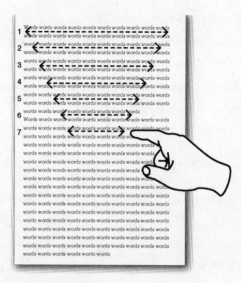

Shortening your short stroke

Vertical drop

Try this useful technique once you are doing the five-word Eye-Hop™. When you are reading newspaper articles, you will know that you can simply drop your eyes down in steps once you have mastered the four-word Eye-Hop™ exercises (see page 130). Most newspaper columns are only five or six words across, so putting your finger down in the middle of the column gives you the whole line! After a little practice, you can simply flow down the column. When you do begin to flow, keep a bit of a sideways curve to your downward stroke. You will find that if you go straight down, you tend to be looking at single words again.

Some people find it easier to pick up two or three lines at a glance once they have become proficient at pattern reading, which we will look at next. Some people like to flow down the page; others like to hop down the page. Whatever works for you is the right way.

Pattern reading

Pattern reading is really what you have been aiming for since the beginning of your journey through SuperReading™. In fact, pattern reading is the quintessential form of reading, which can help you reach your full reading potential. Many people have been amazed by its possibilities for both speed and comprehension.

Before trying the pattern reading technique (this includes the backward S and Z, pages 177–83 below) you **must** be consistently going fairly fast in the four-word Eye-Hop™ (at least ten lines, or 20 hops, in eight seconds). If you are not yet consistent, please wait a few more days in order to have a good experience with this technique.

By the time you have reached this part of the book, you have probably been working your way through the SuperReading™ exercises for at least three or four weeks. You are reading these words with your finger using short stroke. Your comprehension is far better than it was before you bought this book and you've noticed far less drifting off (as described in chapter 2).

You've realized that previewing is extremely cool and useful (see chapter 7). You are getting through material faster and better than ever. Now, you're going to take it up to the next level. Pattern reading is different from what you've been doing up until now, although there are some people who start doing this naturally once they are going fast in the four-word Eye-Hop™. If you do turn out to be one of those people, there are a few pointers that will make pattern reading more powerful for you.

Over the past few weeks you have been preparing your brain to make this leap. Now is the time. You may or may not have noticed, but when you come back to the left column in Eye-Hop™, your finger sweeps toward it and you have actually read the words before you realized it consciously. To put it another way, by the time your finger lands on the word group, you already understand it! While this effect may not happen on every hop, it will begin to occur more often. Take a moment to think about this. Imagine doing your Eye-Hops™. See your finger coming back to the left column. If you understand the words either before your finger touches down or as it touches down, then you get my meaning. In other words, this skill is more advanced than your finger touching down, picking up the words and then moving on, as you were probably doing in the three-word Eye-Hop™.

This means that half the time you have been, in a manner of speaking, reading backward! Yes, backward!

Now it's time to take advantage of this skill to use a technique called backward reading, which is a precursor to the full form of pattern reading.

Backward reading

Backward reading is a method that works really well for some people. It is **not** pattern reading but can be a useful additional skill. If you try the following assignment, you will find out whether or not you can benefit from this reading style. It is good to try backward reading before going on to pattern reading because it will show you that you can read backward, because of the right to left stroke on the Eye-Hop™.

Remember the 21-day rule for reserving judgment from chapter 4. A significant number of people have reported that, at first, backward reading did nothing for them, but later on they tried it again very successfully. Part of this may be that many people simply don't believe that they could possibly read backward. The fact is that when they try it again they have already done more impressive things than reading backward, such as using the memory room (see chapter 13).

ASSIGNMENT

Follow these steps to ensure the highest degree of success in backward reading:

1 Preview two pages, perhaps of this book or a
   newspaper.

2 Read those pages using your finger to trace under the lines from **right** to **left**. You can use short stroke (page 166) if you like.

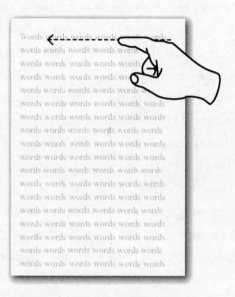

Finger moving right to left

NOTE: Although your finger will be moving from right to left, your eyes will most likely be going from left to right. Somehow this can work quite well. You will find that it works best, the shorter the line. Wide lines make this process more difficult. So choose a book with relatively narrow columns. It would be even better to try backward reading first in a newspaper or magazine. Once you have read the pages, parrot (see chapter 9) to see how much you remember. If your recall is acceptable, then this is a technique you can use from time to time.

I have found that backward reading is very popular with engineers who use the technique to read their engineering journals. It may be that there's something about a logical mind which likes the anomaly of moving in one direction and reading in the other. One theory is that by going in the other direction you are forced to concentrate more on the material. Either way, I suggest starting off with familiar material to see if you get it at all. Most people are amazed that it works. In fact, by moving your finger in the opposite direction in which you are reading, your finger tends to become more of a background object. In some ways it's easier to ignore your finger in favor of seeing the words. I believe this is because you **know** you're not following your finger, so you are free not to let it guide your speed. However, you keep the benefit of letting it move you along because it "forces" you to drop down to the next line and keep some momentum going.

The more you practice backward reading the better you will get at it. Remember that what helps you get going at first is to have narrow columns with familiar text. It may be to your advantage to use backward reading as a review tool (see chapter 10). Once you have seen that this can work, you can move up to pattern reading, which is really the beginning of the ultimate way to read.

Now that you've experienced backward reading it's time to move on to combine the pattern of Eye-Hop™ (chapter 8) with the rhythm of hand pacing (chapter 6)

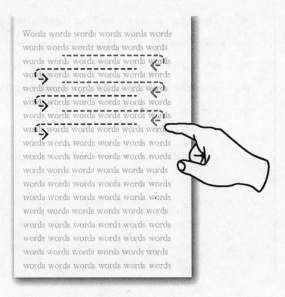

Backward S

for the first form of pattern reading, known as the backward S.

The backward S

I suggest you practice this technique using a children's book to give yourself an easy time at first. See the assignment below for instructions.

ASSIGNMENT

Starting where you normally would on a page, that is

the upper left, preview the material you want to read.

Once you have previewed, go back to the beginning.

You will be using the short stroke idea that you learned

on page 166, but with a twist. When you get to the end

of the first line of the first page, drop down to the next

line and let your finger move from **right** to **left**. As you approach the left margin, drop down a line and move your finger **left** to **right**. Keep moving in this serpentine (snake-like) movement down the page. Go fairly fast. With this method you will observe two things:

1 Your comprehension will be better when you go **faster** (up to a point).
2 You have to trust yourself. This is because you will not be verbalizing much in your head. You will understand without your internal voice giving you nearly as much feedback. You have to simply relax and **let it happen.**

Using this technique will help you to develop some really super speeds. Remember, once you've practiced the backward S technique for a few minutes, if you find your comprehension slipping, you may need to speed up instead of slow down. This method definitely involves faith and trust, because you will not know that you know the material until you parrot (chapter 9).

As you get used to this technique, bear in mind that everyone is different. While pattern reading using the backward S technique, your eyes may follow your finger, or they may ignore your finger completely, or be somewhere in between. For many people, their finger becomes more of a "pacing" tool than a "pointing" tool. Your eyes may be going left to right (>>>) while your finger is going right to left (<<<)! It doesn't matter. Just find out which way works for you, and remember to reserve judgment, as always, for at least 21 days before deciding whether you like pattern reading or not. For most people it's a leap, so you need to keep your mind open and your finger moving!

If you have taken the rep test (in chapter 3), you will know by now the kind of learner you are. If you scored higher than 16 on "digital audio" and tend to repeat things to yourself verbally (this is known as sub-vocalization), pattern reading may possibly be more challenging for you. This is because your brain prefers hearing ideas in your own internal voice and does not willingly give that up. If you are patient and keep practicing pattern reading, using visualization techniques and affirmations to over-come your challenges, you will eventually realize that your sub-vocalization reduces to an efficient level.

WARNING: You will be reading at some rather fast speeds. You will be previewing (chapter 7), so you will know a lot of information. However, there have prob-ably been times in your life when you had to cram for an exam and decided you would read the material really quickly. Most people find that they absorbed very little information that way. Your brain has tracked those times and "knows" you cannot read past a certain speed with any accuracy. You will probably exceed that speed with this method. It's quite possible that your mind will jump to the conclusion that it remembers almost nothing and tell you that when you've finished. Remember that this is impossible because you previewed! Your mind is playing an "old tape," which you can now ignore. Confidently begin to parrot (chapter 9) and soon you will see that you remember impressive amounts of information. The case studies below illustrate this idea. If you give recalling a really good try, and you still cannot recall the material you've just read, then reread it. You may need to adjust your speed (while most people need to slow down, a large number of people actually need to speed up!).

CASE STUDIES

I had an engineer in class who was taking his last test in the final lesson. He did his 20-second preview and then proceeded to read. After reading the passage in about 25 seconds, he was shaking his head. I asked what the problem was. He told me he remembered nothing from the passage. I said, "Just trust yourself. Take the test and remember to smile." About halfway through the questions he had a look of near disbelief on his face. He called me over and said, "This is incredible. I know all the answers. I guess I understood better than I thought!"

He did understand better than he "thought." This is because we're using a different thought process here. It's like watching playing cards flip by very fast. You know you know the cards, but there is no time to say them in your head. You recognize the king, the jack, the four of clubs.

PATTERN READING   **181**

If there were a card that did not belong there you would know that as well. You have been preparing for this for weeks. You are ready. Go for it and let it happen. Just let the story unfold for you. Remember, when you parrot and then review, you will be going even faster. Then reread and go even faster yet. Do it another time and go even faster. Each time you can go faster and understand more completely! Now you're doing it in seconds where before it took minutes!

There was a young woman in one of my classes who was on week five of the course. We were practicing pattern reading. She had brought along a novel to read. There were 18 people in the class, which was a mixture of both students and professionals. As I walked around the room observing my students I noticed a nice smile on her face as she blazed through her novel. She was very absorbed by it. A few minutes later as I came back around I noticed the smile had been replaced by a frown and furrowed brow. I leaned over and asked her what the problem was. She looked up for a moment with a puzzled look on her face. "I don't know what's happened. I was going along just fine, but now my comprehension has just dropped."

I considered for a moment, and asked, "How far did you preview?"

She flipped back a few pages and found the page she had previewed to. Now I knew what to say.

"You've gone past the pages that you previewed. Your comprehension dropped."

She had a look of compete revelation. Her eyes were wide and her mouth was agape. She nodded with understanding and said, "Wow, that previewing really is powerful. Thanks."

I walked off with a bit of a revelation myself. I now knew what to look for when people were pattern reading. I also have confirmation of just how powerful previewing is!

The Z

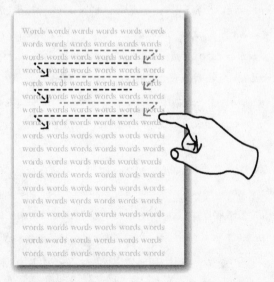

The Z

Another form of pattern reading that some people like is the Z. I would say that about 5 percent of my students prefer this method. This works just like the backward S we have just been looking at, only the movement is more sharply defined. Instead of a flowing motion that floats down the page, the Z is sharp and angular. Try both and see. You will probably like one and dislike the other. There is usually no middle ground.

The problem with the Z is that its sharp angles mean that even at its best, it is not as flexible a pattern as the backward S, and is therefore not as fast. I would recommend the backward S to most people, except perhaps those who operate with their "left brain," such as engineers and lawyers, who might find it more difficult to let go and enjoy the beauty of the flow of the S. However, such people may also find that using the backward S may free up their thinking and expand their potential.

Pattern reading novels

As you will learn for yourself, reading with your finger flowing down the page while you absorb the information is a beautiful experience. Some readers have likened the feeling as being right up there with the best experiences of life. Pattern reading in a novel is particularly satisfying because you will experience the story closer to the "speed of life" and at those speeds you become really "engaged with the page" and filter out the rest of the world. The book not only comes alive, it becomes your universe for a while, so it becomes a true escape, which will transport you to other worlds and realities. After all, isn't that what reading should do for us?

> **ASSIGNMENT**
>
> Pick a simple book to start with. A novel is fine. If you have done your Eye-Hop™ exercises as prescribed, pattern reading should be easy for you. Easy or not, go for it. Relax and let it happen. Thinking about it as you read only gets in the way. Just know that you are doing it right. Your brain will do the rest.

Pattern reading and English as a second language

If English is not your first language, you need to be aware that the challenges of pattern reading will be greater than for those who learned to speak English first. Pattern reading involves massive processing of information as you go down the page. If you recall my warnings about starting with simple material, this goes double for those who did not grow up thinking in English. I recommend starting not only with simple material, but also with simple material in your native language. This all depends upon your level of English development. In my experience of teaching many students for whom English was not their first language, high-speed processing is held back when reading in a second language. It will take more time and more practice. You can do it; you just need to know that it may take anywhere from two to eight weeks longer to become proficient. I know that is quite a wide spread, but there is a huge difference in people's ability to learn languages. The average length I've observed in courses is from two to three weeks, but without knowing an individual it is impossible to be more precise.

My best advice for you if English is your second language is to keep practicing and you will eventually get better and better with pattern reading. If you use visualization techniques and affirmations, this will speed up your progress.

> **ASSIGNMENT**
>
> Try pattern reading in your most comfortable language with simple materials (even children's books). Prove to yourself that it's possible. Once you see that you can handle it, you will know that it's only a matter of time until you can master it in English.

The evolution of pattern reading

The following diagrams show how pattern reading evolves with practice. Over time you may progress through all the stages. The fourth stage is the ultimate reading experience. You are usually picking up multiple lines at a time and your eyes may even be going in other patterns down the page because of line breaks and other factors. It's one of the most difficult things to describe. Once you're really involved in it, especially with a novel, you can lose track of how you're actually progressing down the page. When someone is "engaged with the page," the brain does whatever it needs to in order to follow the story. If you try to be conscious of how you're processing the words, the whole effect can stop. You need to simply "let the book do half the work" and go along for the ride. You are guiding a half-conscious process, so play with it and see how far you can take yourself. What you are aiming for is a beautiful experience where the words flow into your mind, like water in a river. You develop a rhythm and a flow, which feels really good. Reading a novel should feel more like watching a movie.

1   The backward S moves across, down and over the text in a flowing motion. It repeats on the next page where you do a flip turn.

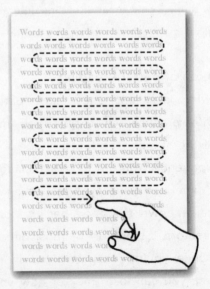

Flowing backward S

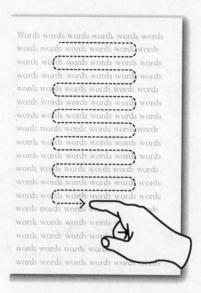

Short stroke backward S

2 The backward S then tightens up with short stroke. You go at the same speed but get down the page faster.

3 The pattern begins to stretch out into a stretched backward S as the brain picks up more and more information when you read multiple lines at once (see page 188).

4 The pattern stretches out further as the brain is able to process entire lines and even paragraphs.

Remember to always keep at least a slight curve to your motion to stop yourself from reading single words again.

Please reserve judgment on these techniques, as they often take time to develop. You may be fortunate to see immediate success with them, but even if that

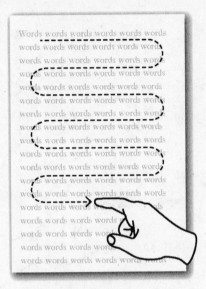

Stretched backward S

Further stretched backward S

happens for you, there's still more development to come. That's why reserving judgment for at least 21 days or 21 times of practice is so valuable. The more open you are to possibilities the more likely it is that those possibilities will manifest.

The half-page speed-up

Once you are well into the four-word Eye-Hop™ you can begin to do something that will keep your reading skills fresh and growing. It's quite a simple technique. There are two reasons to do it and why I am introducing it now. One is to keep from backsliding into reading slowly or even one word at a time again. The other is to keep increasing speed until you reach an upper limit where you simply can't go any further on a particular level of material (such as novels, or a history textbook, or anything). It's like flying a plane up and up. At some point the air will no longer sustain the aircraft. You can't take a plane into outer space. At some point a given person simply cannot absorb information any faster. They have reached what I call their genetic limit. Nobody can read a million words per minute. On their best day, the limit will be somewhere between 100 and 1,000,000 w.p.m. That upper range is not negotiable beyond that point with that material. I've seen people read simple novels faster than 4,000 words per minute with impressive recall. With the enhanced focusing technique (see page 255) I've seen people absorbing information upward of 5,000 to

10,000 w.p.m., though not with the kind of accuracy of pattern reading at 1,000 to 2,000 w.p.m.

Halfway down each page, speed up about 5 percent or a little bit faster than you were going. When you learn about the speed visualization technique in chapter 12 you will discover that you can speed up by 50 to 100 percent and more and not lose any comprehension. In fact, you will often find that your comprehension increases.

To do the half-page speed-up you simply imagine there's a line across the page about halfway down. When you get to the imaginary line, boost your speed a bit. Even though I've suggested an increase of only 5 percent, you may actually speed up 20 percent or more. As long as you are maintaining comprehension you will be fine. Over time those little increases will add up. In the worst case, you won't be backsliding to lower speeds. In the best case, you will see highly significant increases over time with virtually no effort.

You can use this technique both for reading paper materials and on a screen. Let it become second nature and your skills will remain at their peak for years to come.

SUMMARY

- This chapter is about getting better and better. You are progressing from reading one word at a time to absorbing thousands of words per minute.

- Pattern reading uses a "stair step method" of progressing—that is to say you take small steps beyond where you begin and make continual progress until you are pushing the limits of what you will ever be capable of doing.

- Everyone has a genetic limit, but between where you start and where you end up, the difference is remarkable and exciting.

12.

Visualization and affirmation techniques

The visualization and affirmation techniques you will find out about in this chapter are vital to improving your reading performance and will also help you to achieve other goals. Visualization is especially helpful with novels, though it can relate to other reading as well. The ability to hold and manipulate imagery in your head is a powerful tool and will help you to see yourself performing better in many areas. The visualization and affirmation techniques that are especially effective are picture visualization, speed visualization and positive affirmations.

Picture visualization

It has long been known that the human brain is a goal-seeking mechanism that does especially well when the target is well defined. Visualization is the best tool for this as it focuses your mind both consciously and subconsciously. The ability to create a mental image of what you want can be the essential ingredient in any project, and the more detailed and exciting you can make the image, the more precisely your mind will work to create it.

The following assignment will make you a master visualizer. You will need a magazine to practice with, preferably one with plenty of colorful advertisements and visually interesting pages. To get the full benefit repeat the assignment every day for 21 days.

ASSIGNMENT

STEP ONE:

Pick a page and turn it face down. (Ideally get someone else to pick the page for you.) With your eyes closed, hold the page up in front of you.

STEP TWO:

Open your eyes for about a quarter of a second. Close them again straight away. This is called a "visual snapshot."

STEP THREE:

Recall what you saw, out loud. It should only be three or four of the main elements. If you remember much more than that, your eyes were open too long.

STEP FOUR:

Now view the page for five seconds. Recall everything you remember, including what you saw the first time.

STEP FIVE:

View the page for ten seconds. Recall everything you remember, including what you saw the first and second time.

STEP SIX:

Repeat step five twice more until you can remember most of
what is on the page. You will find you are able to remember
large amounts of detail very quickly.

NOTE:

- This is a great exercise to do with someone else. Warning to
  adults: children do very well with this one; you may be outperformed!
- Say what you are looking at when you are viewing
  the page, like an announcer. Example: *There's a woman,
  white blouse, pearl necklace, dark hair, shoulder length,
  parted on my left, gold bracelet—left hand, looking
  to the right* . . .
- When working with a page, read only major titles. Do
  not read text, as this would take too much time. Be aware
  of text, such as how many sections of text are there, any
  colors and where they are on the page. Treat a block
  of text like a picture, for example: *"There's three blocks
  of text at the bottom. The text is white against a blue
  background."*

When you have practiced picture visualization for a few
days, you will notice your skill levels rising. When you
feel this is happening, take one of these images and
begin to change it in your mind. Make an element
twice as big and move it around the page that you see
in your mind's eye. Get it to interact with something
else in the picture. Then, once you master this skill, use

it to visualize **any** goal you set for yourself. Keep building the imagery until you see it as vividly as the magazine pages.

For example, each day, you could spend a couple of minutes seeing yourself reading faster than ever and recalling all that you read. With eyes closed, move your finger at speeds that take you down a page in two seconds. Then speed it up to one second and even faster. It's OK to go really fast in your imagination. You'll be surprised at how soon your brain will begin to respond at similar speeds, especially once you have mastered the four-word Eye-Hop™ (see chapter 8).

Speed visualization

Many top athletes use visualization techniques to enhance their performance. Perhaps not surprisingly, speed visualization can be applied to reading as well as sports. You will be ready to attempt this technique once you are going fast (about ten lines, or 20 hops, in eight seconds) in the four-word Eye-Hop™. The purpose of this technique is to get you reading faster to see that you can pick up more information at higher speeds. This technique will "fool you" into reading faster than normal.

The idea is that you use your finger to read down an imaginary page at lightning speed while imagining that you understand what you read. To be clear, there is really no page in front of you—just a clear table or desk.

This is not the time for weak spirits. This is the time to push yourself and break out of whatever thoughts are holding you back. You want to be pretending to pattern read, getting down each imaginary page in about one second or so.

You can see yourself picking up the information on the imaginary page any way you wish. The knowledge can be going directly into your brain, or it can travel up your arm, or it can play out like a movie in front of you. It does not matter. Just keep telling yourself that you are "getting it." At this point, confidence is more important than the thin veil of reality. When you believe that you are doing it your brain will comply and absorb more information at greater speeds.

It's helpful to think of things you like to do while going fast during this exercise. If you like skiing, or skating, or driving, or running fast, try keeping imagery and emotions from that type of activity in the background while you are doing this. The point is to get used to going faster while feeling good and confident. When you were practicing the half-page speed-up (see page 189) where you increased your reading speed by 5 percent halfway down the page, you will have felt a similar sense of exhilaration and concentration.

You can enhance this technique by playing fast, upbeat music as you are visualizing yourself reading. Instrumental music is best as there are no words to interfere with your concentration. You could try "Popcorn" by Hot Butter or "Flight of the Bumble Bee" by Rimsky-Korsakov.

ASSIGNMENT

Once you are going fast in the four-word Eye-Hop™, get your music ready and perform this technique for about 90 to 120 seconds. Use a book that is of interest to you, but not too highly technical, perhaps a novel or a self-development or business book. Preview and read a chapter to get into the flow of the book. Time yourself to check your speed (words per minute). Then preview another chapter. Halfway through the second chapter (that you just previewed), start the music and do the exercise. When the music ends, or two minutes have passed, turn the music off or down, pick up where you left off and read as fast as you can while maintaining comprehension.

Most people find they naturally go faster because of the speed they just experienced imagining they were reading. Time yourself again, on the first half of the latest chapter and then again on the second half after the exercise. When you finish the chapter, parrot what you remember from the latest chapter (see page 135). You should find that you went much faster and your comprehension was at least as good if not better. If it was not better, do this exercise again in a day or two. Keep doing it until you are going much faster (at least 25 percent) and have equal or better comprehension.

Positive affirmations

Affirmations are statements we make about ourselves. Positive affirmations are usually statements about how we desire to be or how we want to act. They are employed to change the results we are getting in various parts of our lives, by expanding our comfort zones for that area. The most powerful affirmations begin with the words: "I am . . ."

Make a claim for who and what you want to be **now**. Not in the future. The part of your brain you need to reach has little idea of the concept of "future." It only under-stands "now." Therefore, all positive affirmations need to be said in the present tense.

Try these affirmations to improve your reading:

I am a great reader!
I learn things quickly and easily.
I love to read and I'm great at it.

Many people know they are poor readers, and will tell you so. While it's good to have awareness of our weak-nesses, it's another thing to promote them. Each time we do that, we convince our brain it's true and this will lower the electrical activity in the brain, matching results to expectations. After years of claiming a lack of skill, it will take some effort to reverse the situation. The way to do this is simple and effective. However, it will take some determination and persistence. You need to say an affirmation about 100 times a day. You can break this up into 5 sessions of 20 or 4 sessions of 25. Each session will only take a minute or so.

Say your affirmation with emotional feeling. Say it as if you really mean it. Your unconscious mind responds best to highly charged emotion and body movement. Embody these affirmations. Make them a part of you; especially those that stick in your throat or cause you dismay. Reading them silently is OK too, but saying them aloud adds more sense and feeling to the message.

Try looking at yourself in the mirror from time to time when you say your affirmations. Look right into your own eyes and say, "I am a great reader," or whatever your affirmation is. This will drive it deeply into your mind. Think about it—you may well have said or thought you were a poor reader hundreds or thousands of times. It will take at least that many repetitions of your affirmation to reverse the programming. However, saying more than 100 a day will not yield much better results. Saying 3,000 in a row is not nearly as effective as saying 20 every couple of hours each day over a month. The value of continually reminding yourself over time cannot be underestimated.

The following positive affirmations are intended to address any underlying mental attitudes that would hold you back from either attaining or maintaining your SuperReading™ skills. (I've provided lots of affirmations and some are variations on a theme which might seem slightly repetitious, but I've done this so you can find just the right ones to address your needs.) Read through the list to choose the ones that you want to focus on. If any seem hard to say, or silly or give you a strange reaction, they may have touched a nerve connected to a learning block. To overcome the block faster, say that particular affirmation over and over again.

Ideas and facts flow to me from the page.
I recall what I read easily and effortlessly.
I like reading. I flow along in a rhythmic motion,
absorbing information as I go.
Understanding comes easily to me.
I do really well in tests, for I have tested myself
more thoroughly than any teacher could.
When taking tests, I know that I know the material.
I deserve to be a great reader.
I relax and let the words flow into my mind.
As my finger sweeps across the page, I understand
and remember what I read.
I am a great student.
I am a great learner.
My reading skills get better and better every day.
Each time I read, my comprehension gets better
and better.
I like the feeling of having read well.
I allow myself to be the superb reader that I am.
There is so much good information around that I
am thankful for having the gift of great reading.
Reading is fun for me and I get better at it every day.

I go easy on myself, for I know that some days are
better than others when it comes to mental
activities.

I appreciate the advantage of previewing and allow
myself those rewards.

I enjoy reading stories. It's like watching a movie
where I control the speed.

My mind works beautifully at giving me the
knowledge I need.

I trust that I get all I need when I read.

When I read, my finger sweeps across the page,
pulling the meaning into my mind.

It's OK for me to be a great reader.

I have a great brain and great skills. No wonder
I'm such a great reader.

Reading for me is easy. I know what to do and I do
it well.

All subjects are accessible to me, for I know how
to learn.

When I read, it's OK not to get it all the first time
around. I am aware there is more, and I'll pick it
up next time.

I am an effective reader. I make good use of my time.

I know what great reading is, and I know I can do it.

I am a great reader.

I recall what I read with ease and accuracy.

I like reading rhythmically, absorbing facts as I go.

Understanding comes naturally to me now.

I am prepared to take tests, having thoroughly
tested myself.

I am relaxed when taking tests, because I know
that I know the material.

I claim my right to be a great reader.

I feel relaxed as the words flow into my mind.

Using my finger to read helps me to understand
and recall information.

I enjoy previewing material.

I love learning.

My reading skills improve each day.

Each time I read, my comprehension improves.

I allow myself to be a great reader.

Reading boosts my confidence.

Reading has become my favorite activity.

I am kind to myself, because some days are better
than others.

I appreciate previewing and allow myself its rewards.

I enjoy reading stories. I can control the pace to
suit myself.

My mind works efficiently.

I trust that when I read I pick up all the key facts.

Reading is now such fun for me.

I get pleasure from doing such a great job at reading.

It's OK if I struggle at first to understand a book. I
am a super reader.

I am intelligent and a brilliant reader.

Reading for me is rewarding because I learn so much.

When I read, I understand most of the text the first
time. I pick up the rest when I review what I have
read.

My efficient reading saves me time.
I know what it takes to be a great reader, and I know I am one.
Nobody is perfect, including authors and editors. I forgive them for poor writing and organization. I use my skills to understand their valuable ideas.
I use my reading skills to continually empower myself and others.
All I need to learn is accessible to me.
Written information is available to me faster and better every day.
With each passing day, I become a better and better reader.
I am thankful for my abilities, and I rejoice in using them.
It feels good to do things that enhance the quality of my life.
I take positive advantage of ideas and opportunities.
I have fun reading and learning about the important things in life.
I naturally attract the information and knowledge I need.
I see that reading well is a skill I can learn and use.
I apply my skills and grow stronger and better every day.
I accept my new skills and welcome them into my life.
I am relaxed and confident when I read.
I accept my reading skills, knowing there is always room for growth.

It's OK for me to practice and become a great reader.
I pick up good ideas when I read and incorporate
them into my life.
I practice my new skills and read better and better
every day.
I like myself regardless of practicing my exercises.
I realize reading is a key to my future and I
consistently invest time in my skills.
I like myself when I read.
A calm, relaxed feeling comes over me when I read.
It's simple becoming a great reader and I become a
better reader all the time.
My ability to learn and remember grows and grows.
Reading and recalling becomes easier and easier
for me.
I like the feeling of smoothly reading across the
lines; the words flowing into my mind.
Parroting is fun for me. The more I parrot, the
better I get. Parroting gives me more confidence
every time.
I always know where I stand.
Whatever level I'm at is OK. I know great reading
is within my reach.
I continually move toward being a better reader
all the time.
No matter how I do on any given day, I see myself
as a great reader and learner.
Nobody does their personal best every day; I like the
direction in which my reading skills are moving.

ASSIGNMENT

Read the affirmations above out loud. Judge how each one makes you feel. Choose three of them—one that feels really good when you say it, one that makes you uncomfortable when you say it, and one that addresses a particular challenge you have. Do each one 100 times a day in five sets of 20, spread out during your day, like when you awake, after breakfast, before lunch, before dinner, before bedtime. Say them with feeling (win that acting award!). Embody them (through repetition and emotion).

Work on no more than three affirmations at a time. You can work on one, two or three affirmations at any one time. Do an affirmation for at least 21 days. Once you feel it's embodied and you have accepted it or the "problem" associated with it is resolved, you may replace it with a new one.

NOTE: Affirmations may seem irrelevant or ridiculous to you. However, they can be very powerful. Remember that we do talk to ourselves subconsciously all day long, and that part of our subconscious brain does listen to what we say. So reserve judgment for at least 21 days and do yourself a favor.

Affirmations for speakers of English as a second language

If your first language is not English, you may want to consider saying affirmations in your first language. The patterns and thoughts you are overcoming are probably from the first eight years of your life. Whatever language you formed those ideas in may be the one to reverse them with. It depends on how well you think in English. If your immediate reaction to situations has you thinking in your first language, then that's probably the one to go with.

You can also do affirmations in both languages. Try both and see over time which has the most impact for you. Just be aware that saying affirmations in different languages may have different success rates.

ASSIGNMENT

Write out an affirmation that excites you and changes your thinking about yourself in a positive way. Be sure it is positive and refers to now and not the future. There should be no hint of the words: no, not, don't, won't, will, going to, will be, want. Do use the words "I am" to begin your affirmation. For example, "I am a great reader."

SUMMARY

- The ability to see what you want to accomplish is paramount to achieving it.

- Using picture visualization will bring your goal of being a super reader closer.

- Speed visualization allows you to experience faster reading with high comprehension by building momentum.

- Affirmations are an excellent tool for helping you to address false or unhelpful beliefs which hold back your progress and growth.

PART FOUR:

Further Techniques and Strategies

13.

Learning and memory

When we begin to turn on the real power of the brain, most of the challenges of learning limitations such as dyslexia fade away. In this chapter we will look at ways of learning and improving the memory that make reading more fun and accessible to all kinds of learners.

I had a 21-year-old student who had been labeled as dyslexic since primary school. In the third lesson of the course, he jumped up and yelled out, "I understand this! This is amazing—I just read this and I understand it! This has never happened before. Wow! I can read. I can really read!"

"Education is not the filling of a pail—but the lighting of a fire."

WILLIAM BUTLER YEATS

He was so excited that it took him a couple of minutes to calm down. He slapped his hand to his head and started talking about all the years of going to special schools and tutors and struggling so hard. Now it was so easy. At these schools they were trying to get him to think; SuperReading™ got him to read! The point is that most learning disabilities are disabling because the person is trying to do the task with only one part of their brain—the troubled part. Once you get more of the brain involved, the appropriate parts take over and do the job. Teamwork is the key. So do not label yourself. Just let your brain figure out a way as you go. You certainly will not do yourself any harm if you learn how to read fast!

A study of SuperReading™ was undertaken at London South Bank University in 2008. The findings showed that indeed dyslexic adults saw significant improvement in their reading abilities. Surprising to the experimenter, those students with the lowest scores to begin with saw the greatest percentage increase in their reading abilities. Most of them became better than non-dyslexic readers. While they were hopeful for some improvement, becoming a better reader than a non-dyslexic reader was more than most of them had hoped for.

NOTE: A key to learning is focus. Staying in focus on your subject leads to learning so when you are studying, stick to one subject at a time. When you have been reading about algebra, for example, parrot that information (see chapter 9) and then take a break. Relax and recharge by meditating, working out, enjoying a conversation or whatever you wish. Now move on to history or whatever subject you wish to tackle next. This is such an important part of SuperReading™ that the next chapter (chapter 14) is devoted to looking at ways to focus your mind to help your reading efforts.

CASE STUDIES

Chris, age 11, was one of the poorest readers I had ever come across. His mother told me that Chris had been seen by more than a dozen reading experts. When he took his first test, where most of the children in the class finished in less than three minutes, it took Chris nearly eight minutes. He could not answer a single question in the quiz. The next week he was still taking over six minutes to read, while the other children were mostly under the two-minute mark. Chris could now answer one question while the others were averaging seven or eight. Four weeks later there was not much improvement and I was concerned he would drop out. I gave my "Hang in there" speech to the whole class, targeting Chris, who by this time was the only one who really needed it. I couldn't tell if I had reached him, as he had never made eye contact with me.

The next time we tested, something amazing happened. Chris's reading time dropped to just under three minutes. He correctly answered six out of ten questions. His reading effectiveness score (see chapter 5) skyrocketed. He looked me in the eye for the first time. Hesitantly, he asked, "Mr. Cole, is this really my reading score?" I came over and looked at his time, answers and graph. "Yes. That's correct." What happened next is something I will always remember. He looked up at me with what can only be described as an "ear-to-ear grin." I truly believe that was a turning point in his young life. From that moment on he was a different person. He began to fully participate in the class and interact with the other students.

At the end of the course Chris's mother approached me and thanked me profusely. She said that all his teachers reported a profound change in his attitude and performance. She felt that within another few weeks he would become the best reader in his class. And he did.

In that same course was a young woman of about 14. When she started, she presented herself as a bit of an airhead. She laughingly put herself down, reveling in her stupidity and "ditziness," which I think she felt would somehow appeal to the boys in the class. This behavior continued for about three or four weeks. Then something profound happened. As her test scores rose from about 50 to over 300, her attitude toward herself changed. Once she had tested twice at that level and saw it was real, she dropped the façade. Suddenly she looked quite studious and focused. She almost looked like a different person and she was certainly behaving differently. Her mother told me, "I can't believe the change. Her marks are higher at school and she actually sits down to do her homework without a fuss. Last Saturday I found her lying on her bed reading a book." I replied, "That's great." Her mother replied, "You don't understand. This is a kid who never picked up a book in her life. She could have been out goofing around, but she decided to stay home and read. Whatever you're doing here, keep doing it. And thanks."

I've told these stories here because I believe true learning should come from a love of learning. It's really asking a lot from people to love something they hate to do because it's painful. When we can read and have some fun with it, as I will show you later in this chapter, then learning comes about naturally.

Reading ability and intelligence

I've been asked if reading ability reflects intelligence. I believe it does to some degree but not as much as you might imagine. Of course you must have at least a few brain cells firing to understand what you read. If we were to measure intelligence by how much a person can recall from what they've read, then my graduates are geniuses! When you can go on and on about a book you read ages ago, people will believe that you are very intelligent too. I prefer to say that this course will make you look as intelligent as you really are, or more so!

There is a myth that we can only store a limited amount of information in our brains. Nothing could be further from the truth, **unless** you believe it. Then your brain will act accordingly. Remember: "Whether you think you can, or whether you think you can't, you're probably right!" The human brain has about one hundred billion neurons, or brain cells. The possible number of neural connections in one human brain is far greater than the number of atoms in the known universe! So don't worry about running out of storage space. Your brain's true capacity is greater than you'll ever need. It's not about storage; it's about retrieval. This is where memory techniques come into play. Look back to chapter 10, where you learned some simple techniques for helping retrieval and recall, ranging from using emotion to spaced repetition.

Making learning fun and interactive

One of the best ways to learn is to make your learning fun. Make up games. Get physical and act out what's going on. Use all your senses to learn—or as many as are appropriate. Use your imagination to be silly and outrageous. Explain what you are learning to someone else; even if they are not actually there. You could even look in the mirror and explain it to yourself.

The saying goes, "If you really want to understand something, teach it to someone else." This is because teaching is the ultimate form of parroting (see chapter 9).

It's parroting with more feedback and questions! If you can't answer the questions, that tells you to go back and review (see chapter 10). And don't be shy. If there's something you don't know, or can't find again, revel in it. If you're blocked from understanding a piece of knowledge, there's probably a good reason for it. It usually indicates an unconscious cause for the blockage. There may be a hidden need your unconscious mind has for keeping you from understanding or even acknowledging it. Forcing yourself to gain that understanding can result in a breakthrough in your life. We all live in comfort zones. The mechanisms behind the comfort zones will use any means to hide information from us that is contrary to the hidden beliefs that support the nonresourceful belief. When a question in a textbook or a comment from an author brings it to our conscious attention, we have a small window of opportunity to look at it and realize a truth that has eluded us. An example would be reading an article that mentions follow-through. You have been told this is an area you need to work on. You don't recall reading the comment and go hunting for it. However, you just can't locate it. You scan a couple of times but it's just not jumping out at you. Most people would give up and let it go. The opportunity vanishes. They have missed out on a vital key to their success. Why? Because some destructive pattern needs them to be unaware of the trend they have not to follow-through. They remain at a low level of success. So when this kind of opportunity comes along, go for it!

Questions are an important part of learning. Use the magnetic questions you first encountered in chapter 7 (remember Who, What, When, Where, Why and How?). In particular, use Why and How a lot. These are the ones that really test your knowledge and understanding.

And importantly, do not judge yourself. Judging leads to bad feelings and lower performance. Whatever happens, just accept it and see yourself doing better in the future. Remember: "There is no failure, only feedback." In fact, failure is fine. It is just another form of parroting. It tells you there are more things you have to do. And "giving up" is not one of them!

ASSIGNMENT

Before you begin to learn something new, stop and ask yourself, "What can I do to make this fun and interactive?" If you have no great answer to this question, think of one and do it, before you start to learn. If you need help in coming up with something, read on. Set a timer and see how much information you can absorb before the bell rings. If you learned six facts in two minutes, now try learning seven facts in two minutes. Or, imagine there are several people there with you and they are going to ask you questions. You learn as much as you can in a specific amount of time and pretend to answer their questions. Or imagine you are on a game show and you have to read an article and know at least five facts, and earn more money for all the facts you remember beyond five. The novelty of these activities will increase your attentiveness and recall. Use your imagination and come up with different scenarios.

Top tips for facilitating learning

Getting interested

When you are reading, your body language is important if you want to make the most of it. Have you ever seen somebody sitting at a table, with their head leaning against their hand at an odd angle? If you were selling something to this person, would you think that they were paying attention? Not a chance. If you sit to read in such a position of noninterest do you think that your brain can really be paying attention to what you are reading? It cannot. Pay attention to how you are sitting. Sit in the way that you would when you are keenly interested in something and your brain will follow along and absorb more information more quickly. Be truly interactive. Lean forward, keep your eyes wide open, have a happy or excited expression on your face and nod approvingly when you begin. You will find more on this in chapter 14 ("Artificial interest" on page 247).

Learning anomalies

Sometimes when we are learning a new skill or technique our abilities temporarily suffer. This is natural. Take any skill you are already familiar with, such as writing. What if you had to write with your other hand? Would that make a difference? Even signing your name would be very difficult and you could not copy your own signature unless you practiced a lot. What about writing in the dark or blindfolded? Would that decrease your skill? Of course it would. With practice and determination, could you build up your skills again? The answer is yes, of course. Be aware of this when learning a new skill and your ability to overcome minor dips in performance will not upset you. You will know by now the importance of reserving judgment (chapter 4) and you should just keep forging ahead until your abilities catch up again.

Attitude

Another thing that facilitates learning is attitude. Being happy and feeling good opens centers of the brain that are important to effective learning. The easiest ways to get happier and therefore facilitate better learning are through smiling and imagery. Simply smiling, or laughing lightly, relaxes the body and the mind, and leads to pushing out negative mind chatter. The other thing that works well if your mind won't shut off is the use of vivid imagery, which was looked at in detail in chapter 12. Using imagery brings your right brain into play. Your right brain controls much of what you do, and is relatively non-judgmental. When the right brain is to the fore you can perform without the usual critical judgment that might get in your way.

My favorite way to clear the mind and adjust your attitude is called alphabet animals, a simple way to lift your mood and raise a smile, to put yourself in the right frame of mind for effective learning. This technique also works well to help you deal with negative feelings at any time.

ASSIGNMENT

Pick any letter of the alphabet. Think of an animal beginning with that letter. See that animal in your mind, either with your eyes open or closed. Get the animal to start moving. See it run or fly. See it go up a tree. Now see it dancing on a tree branch. Perhaps it's dancing a jig. Give it a top hat and tails—bright pink! And a green polka-dot tie. And now give it a cane. Set the scene to music in your mind—perhaps "Puttin' on the Ritz." Now get the animal to jump off the tree into a bucket of bright red paint. Its head pops up and the animal sticks its tongue out at you.

Now if you really managed to visualize that, you should be feeling pretty lighthearted by now and ready to do some effective learning.

Next time you try alphabet animals you can either go into a lot of detail with your animal or get it to interact with other things (for example, you could see a 6-foot penguin in New York City) or other animals. Once you've done a couple of these, they shouldn't take more than half a minute, you will find your mood will lift and a smile will come to your face. Sometimes just thinking about them can instantly lighten your mood.

The brain scan experiment

In the early 2000s I watched a TV documentary about a university experiment that got me jumping up and down with excitement. It seemed to prove convincingly that belief, which is closely tied to attitude, affects performance.

The TV screen was split into three parts. The middle and largest section showed a man sitting in a room at a table. On the table were a variety of puzzles that were numbered for clear identity. In the upper left corner of the TV screen was a shot of the room next door. In the room were two experimenters, separated from the man at the table by a one-way mirror (they could see him, but he could not see them).

The man was sitting under a portable MRI (magnetic resonance imaging) scanning machine. It was lowered down so it could take scans of his brain while still allowing him to see the table in front of him. In the upper right corner of the TV screen was the readout from the MRI. It showed a top-down view of his brain. Whenever electrical activity increased, the computer displayed the color red in that location. The experimenters got him relaxed and then asked him questions to determine his "at rest" electrical activity. They put three groups of people through this experiment. The first group was used to establish base levels of activity while at rest and when solving puzzles. They gathered data from a large group of people to see how much time it took to solve the various puzzles and to see which parts of the brain worked on the various kinds of problems. The first group, the control group, gave them all that basic information.

When one of the experimenters turned on the microphone, there was an audible "CLICK" sound. The subject also heard the "CLICK" sound when the microphone was turned off.

CLICK (on)

Experimenter: "OK, Frank, do you see the puzzle near the number 1 on the table?"

Frank: "Yes."

Experimenter: "Good. In a moment, when I say 'Go,' start solving that puzzle. When you are finished, raise your hand. We will be timing you. Do you understand?"

Frank: "Yes."

Experimenter: "Very good. Ready . . . begin."

CLICK (off)

Frank worked on the puzzle and when he finished, raised his hand.

CLICK (on)

Experimenter: "OK. Now do the same with Puzzle 2. Raise your hand when you finish. Begin."

CLICK (off)

Frank worked on Puzzle 2 and when he finished, raised his hand.

CLICK (on)

Experimenter: "OK. Now do the same with Puzzle 3. Raise your hand when you finish. Begin."

CLICK (off)

The experiment continued on through about ten different puzzles. This gave the experimenters a really good idea of how long it took to solve the puzzles and which parts of the brain were called into play. As the subjects went along, their electrical activity rose in response to the problem solving. We could see the rise displayed in red on the monitor from the scan.

Now the experimenters were ready to play with people's minds a bit . . .

The second group they ran through their paces was the positive group. The experiment started off the same as the control group's. For the first four puzzles everything was the same. Then something different happened.

CLICK (on)

Experimenter: "OK, Jeffrey. Now do the same with Puzzle 5. Raise your hand when you finish. Begin."

But there was no CLICK OFF!

The subject, someone named Jeffrey, waited a couple of seconds and then began to work on Puzzle 5.

After a little while the two experimenters in the hidden booth had a conversation, which Jeffrey could hear clearly, that went something like this:

Experimenter 1: "Wow, this guy is really smart!"
Experimenter 2: "I know, he's very clever. He's solving these puzzles faster than anyone I've seen."
Experimenter 1: "I think we can get out of here early tonight."
Experimenter 2: "Great! Want to stop off for a coffee?"
Experimenter 1: "Sure. Let's see if he keeps going like this."

Jeffrey solves Puzzle 5 and raises his hand. There's a CLICK but he doesn't hear anything. There's a couple more CLICKS and he finally hears the experimenter's voice. The experimenter sounds a bit put off.

Experimenter: "O—OK Jeffrey, good. Now do the same thing with Puzzle 6. Begin."
CLICK (off)

Jeffrey now realizes that he was not supposed to hear that conversation between the two experimenters. He thinks they accidentally left the microphone on. What Jeffrey does not know is that it was all part of the plan. They were actors who had a carefully written script to give the impression that they were really impressed with him.

When he first heard their conversation the electrical

activity in his brain increased. When Jeffrey started on Puzzle 7 he was feeling really confident. His electrical activity shot up and on the monitor we could see areas of his brain lighting up in red that had not shown any activity before. He outperformed the control group and got even better on Puzzle 8. His brain was lighting up like crazy! Jeffrey believed in himself because of the experimenters' conversation and his performance went through the roof.

It was at this point that I realized how important this experiment was. It showed in graphic form that our brain works harder and better when we believe in ourselves. Jeffrey was cleverer when he believed he was clever!

The experiment did not stop there. There was a third group—the negative group. It went something like this:

CLICK (on)
Experimenter 1: "OK, Sam. Now do the same with Puzzle 5. Raise your hand when you finish. Begin."
But there was no CLICK OFF!
The subject, someone named Sam, waited a couple of seconds and then began to work on Puzzle 5. After a little while the two experimenters in the hidden booth had a conversation that went something like this:
Experimenter 1: "Jeez, where do they find these people?"
Experimenter 2: "I know. This guy is like Forrest Gump or something."

Experimenter 1: "It's like watching paint dry."

Experimenter 2: "At this rate we'll be here all night. I'd better call my wife."

Experimenter 1: [sigh] "Yeah . . ."

The result was amazing. In real time you could actually see the red disappearing from the monitor. The scan revealed Sam's brain actually shutting down. The patterns went back to base level where he was sitting waiting to begin. The negative comments from the experimenters just sucked the life out of poor Sam. He took longer than the control group and couldn't even solve some of the puzzles. It was heartbreaking to watch. Fortunately, when the negative group finished, the whole scheme was revealed to them so they didn't go home thinking they were deficient. Their first few scores were shown to them and compared with the control group, so they could see they were "normal."

I share these results with you to demonstrate that how we view ourselves directly affects our ability to perform. By treating ourselves well we stand a better chance of increasing performance. This is related to another important subject: affirmations (see page 198).

Improving your memory

We now move on to the core section of this chapter—finding the keys to improving your memory. Memory is a fascinating subject. Your brain is holding on to millions and millions of pieces of information. It's all in there somewhere. The big question is: "Where on earth is it?" Just imagine—you can have instant access to so many strange and bizarre facts. For example, think about . . . your refrigerator. What are you experiencing now? Are you seeing what's inside? Are you seeing the outside? Are you recalling the contents? A minute ago those facts were not in your consciousness. Now they are. In an hour they probably will not be in your consciousness again. We store so much information, but the key is not storage; it is retrieval and recall. The following elements of repetition, emotion, imagination, motion and association are known as the five keys to memory.

We have already touched on this subject in chapter 10 because memory techniques play a significant role in reviewing. Some of this information may already seem familiar, but that's OK, because the first key to memory is repetition!

Memory testing

Before we go on to discover the keys to memory, it would be interesting to test your memory skills as they are now. The best way to test your memory is with the help of another person. Get them to go to the list on the next page and read each word aloud after saying its number, starting with number 1. Ask them to count to five silently and continue with number 2, and so on.

When they get to number 20, wait five seconds and then take a minute to discuss between you something unrelated to the list, like your favorite movies, TV shows or books. After one minute, begin writing the words you remember by their number in a list, starting with the first word. If you cannot remember which number a word goes with, just write it down by any open number. Take no more than three minutes for writing your answers down.

After that, get the person to read the list back to you, saying both the number and the word. Circle the words that you got correct by their number. Those are worth 5 points. Words from the list that are by the wrong number are worth 1 point. Your answers may be plural or singular and spelling does not matter.

Memory test 1

Read aloud clearly and carefully. Say the number and the word; wait five seconds, go to the next word.

1. Mattress
2. Clarinet
3. Peanut
4. Doughnut
5. Car
6. Pencil
7. Tape
8. Eagle
9. Shoe
10. Cloud

11. Tree
12. Rainbow
13. Ladder
14. Dairy
15. Monitor
16. Fork
17. Shirt
18. Dream
19. Brush
20. Crayon

Allow five seconds after the last word, and then have a conversation for one minute. After that minute, it is time to write the answers down against the numbers, writing the first word first.

The five keys to memory

1 I have just said that the first key to memory is **repetition**. The more you repeat something, the more likely you are to remember it. Do you remember five times five? How about seven times seven? Of course you do. You cannot even keep the answers out of your head. Four times four? These facts are so deeply ingrained by repetition that you will always remember them. But how about 19 times 19? Probably nothing comes to mind. This is because there was not enough repetition in that case, since most people do not learn their times tables beyond 10 or 12. We see then that multiple exposures to information lead to permanent recall. The same thing is true when we read. The more times we see or experience the message, the more likely we are to recall it.

2 The next key to memory is **emotion**. We tend to remember that to which we have reacted with high levels of emotion. Take a minute to recall your most vivid memories. You will find that there is some emotional reaction when you recall them. The emotion served to seal in the memory. You can use this to your advantage by getting emotionally excited about specific things you wish to learn.

Even if you are acting, your brain cannot tell the difference. Your body will react as if the emotions are "real." Aristotle knew all about this. When he came to a critically important fact he wished a student to remember he would slap them across their face! Rest assured there are more reasonable methods of eliciting emotions and recalling information. One example is mental shouting where you see yourself standing on a table in an expensive restaurant, loudly shouting out the information you wish to recall. Shout it out several times in your mind.

3   The third key to memory is **imagination**. As Albert Einstein said, "Imagination is more important than knowledge." If you want to remember things really well, you have to engage your brain with your imagination. Words are simply sounds. These sounds only have meaning because we all agree to their meaning. The word "boat" could just as easily mean "fence" if we all agreed to change it. The things that transcend words are pictures and when we use pictures we use our imagination. No matter what you call a baby, we all know what one looks like and most of us react the same way upon seeing one. When we see a cute baby we react emotionally first, then the word comes to us. You can enhance memory using imagination by exaggerating something or by making it very silly. For example, if you need to recall a catfish, vividly see one swimming

around the room with you. Now make it 3 yards long. Now make it say "meow" very loudly as it swims through the air. Physically grab its tail and hold on as it struggles to free itself. Act this out right now. Have it turn its head and hiss at you like a cat! Now you will remember "catfish." Reinforce it by saying out loud, "Wow, this catfish can struggle!"

4   The fourth key to memory is **motion**. This has just been demonstrated with the catfish example above. Our eyes and brains are hardwired to respond to motion. We notice things that move, so make objects move in order to recall them better. More of your brain comes into play when you create action. Static objects tend to fade into the background and are forgettable. Imagine that you're visiting a zoo. You are looking at a herd of antelope simply standing there munching the plants. You're about to move on to the next pen. If you were recalling your day at the zoo, these antelope would not have been mentioned. Suddenly one of the antelope starts jumping up and down and running madly in circles. It jumps over several of the other antelope and starts spinning round. Now the antelope have become one of the highlights of the day and may even be the first thing you talk about. Why? Because of motion. Its movements made it special and helped you to remember them.

5   The fifth key is **association**. Associate the item you want to remember with something you already

know. What does it remind you of? Creatively link the item with something you know really well. For example, if you had to remember some information about a phone tree, you could link it with a real tree near your home or work.

One way to sum this up is to say that if you experience **movement**, **associate** with what you want to recall, **repeat** the process in some **imaginative** way with **emotion**, you will have no choice but to **remember** a piece of information! Now you have an acronym to remember: **M.A.R.I.E**:

MOVEMENT and
ASSOCIATION
REPEATED,
IMAGINED with
EMOTION

Memories are made permanent through repetition, but interestingly, the more emotions, movement and imagination you use, the less repetition you need! And of these, emotion is especially powerful. Emotion really seals in a memory. Look at your earliest life memories. They almost always have strong emotion attached to them. This is not coincidence. This is how your brain works. Use it. And, most of all, have fun when you use it.

The Roman room

The Roman room memory technique dates back to the ancient days of the Roman Empire, when scholars used the objects in a room to remember items of importance. This technique will help you remember things in a particular order. It's a very easy system to learn, stands alone and does not interfere with other memory techniques you may use.

How to do the Roman room

The illustration below shows one of five elements of a kitchen including the dishwasher and the sink. For the first exercise you will use this area to help you remember a list of items. You will see the whole kitchen on the next page and will progress to remembering all 20 objects in the room.

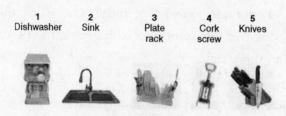

1 Dishwasher	**2** Sink	**3** Plate rack	**4** Cork screw	**5** Knives

A typical kitchen area

The procedure is to memorize the objects along each wall of our sample room (above) in the correct numerical order. You will always use them in this order. The first object to remember is the dishwasher. Imagine the dishwasher racks moving backward and forward and say to yourself "dishwasher." The next object is the sink. Say that it is a sink and see the swiveling tap, then do the plate rack, the corkscrew and finally the set of knives. The point of memorising these objects is to establish a permanent base of 20 "slots" where you will be associating other "items" you wish to remember for work, school or anything else. In other words, this room (see full room on page 236) is something you keep in your head just as it is, and from time to time you use it to remember lists of things that become attached to it. The room is a tool you use like file folders in a drawer to keep papers in a specific order so you can find them. Instead of folders, you have objects (dishwasher, sink, plate rack, corkscrew, knives).

Now, comes the practical bit: let's say you're going to the supermarket. You need five items. You have no paper. No problem!

The idea is to creatively merge an object in the kitchen with whatever it is you want to recall. You will do this by making the two things interact with each other using the following three steps:

Verbalize: say the first word you need to recall over and over again (repetition) out loud if possible.

Exaggerate: make the thing to remember bigger, brighter than it really is or imagine many of them. Make it unusual, such that if you saw one like this it would make a big impression on you.

Movement: we pay more attention to things that move than things that are still. This is why we use our finger (hand pacing, which we learned about in chapter 6) when we read. If there is action in your interaction you will recall the thing more easily.

In our example, the first item to remember on your shopping list is bread. See the bread (sliced or a loaf) thrown into the dishwasher. Perhaps the spray arm is spinning the bread around. Say to yourself: "The dishwasher is spinning the bread."

Next in the kitchen is the sink. Your next shopping item is facial tissue. See yourself pulling tissues out of the box and stuffing them into the sink. Or perhaps the sink is sneezing and you hand it a tissue. It blows its nose. Think of something totally outrageous. That way you will remember! Tell yourself that the tissues are helping the sink.

Next is the plate rack. You need some beach sandals and you have heard they are on special offer. How would you get the plate rack to interact with the beach sandals? Make it happen and tell yourself what you are creating.

Next is the corkscrew. Merge the corkscrew with peanut butter. Spread it on. Then carefully lick the corkscrew and feel the sticky peanut butter. Say to yourself that you are licking peanut butter off the corkscrew.

Last are the knives. You need to buy plastic cups. See yourself stabbing white plastic cups with the knives. Say what you are creating and seeing.

If you have more than five items to remember, keep going around the room. Your limit is 20 items. Experience shows that most lists you make will have fewer than 20 items.

ASSIGNMENT

The best strategy to memorize the room is to spend two minutes with a section of it about five times a day. Look at it, say it, close your eyes and repeat it verbally. Once you have it memorized, see if you can quiz yourself

| 20 Fridge | 1 Dishwasher | 2 Sink | 3 Plate rack | 4 Cork screw | 5 Knives | 6 Spice rack |

| 19 Dryer | | | 7 Stove |

| 18 Microwave | 13.2 | | 8 Kettle |

| 17 Cookies | | | 9 Toaster |

| 16 Bin | 15 Scales | 14 Honey pot | 13 Whisk | 12 Blender | 11 Bread | 10 Phone |

The Roman room

going backward around the section of the room. Eventually you need to memorize all 20 objects in the room, and know which object belongs on which wall. It is also very helpful to learn which numbers go with which objects.

Other rooms

You can also use your own room or rooms with this technique. I strongly suggest using five objects per space (wall or central area). The reason for always having five objects is for consistency. It makes remembering the number of each object easier and it is less confusing to have a consistent number of objects in each group as you go around. In that way, you are always sure when you get to a corner what number you are on. I also suggest four areas per room. In other words, the basic layout of rooms is fairly consistent; only the objects change from room to room.

If you are using a room from your life (bedroom, kitchen, den, office, the room you grew up in) and there are not enough objects in a given space, then simply add one in using your imagination. Just tell yourself that that object is now there. For example, along a wall in your bedroom is a lamp, chair, a window and a chest of drawers. That's only four objects. In your mind, you could imagine that next to the chest is a picture of a tree, or a cuckoo clock, or a trophy, or a plant.

HINT: Be sure not to duplicate objects, either in the

same room or in any of your rooms. For example, having a recliner in two of your rooms would potentially be confusing. Or having two stereo speakers in the same room could cause uncertainty as to which one was associated with which object to remember.

THOUGHT: Most people are literally amazed at how effective and easy this technique is for remembering things. You put a few seconds of creative work into each association and then let it go. When you come back to the beginning the thing you need to remember just pops out at you, as clear as can be.

HOPE: Memorising a room is really easy. All it takes is a bit of repetition. Just spend a minute or two here and there going over one section of five objects. It should not take more than about 40 minutes to memorize a room this way. Once you have it, you will always have it. Memorize the numerical position as well for instant access to any object in the room. For example, if someone asked me what the third longest river in the world is, I would think of the third object in the room, the plate rack. When thinking about rivers, I would access that particular information. In this case, it's "yanking" a dish from the rack. Yanking reminds me of "Yang," short for the Yangtze (*Yang see*). In about one to two seconds I would be saying the answer. No matter which river I might be asked about, it would only take a second or two to know the answer, assuming I have memorized the numerical position of each object.

ASSIGNMENT

Use the Roman room technique to remember a shopping list (or similar) every time you get the chance.

Textbooks

While we are on the subject of learning, it would seem the right moment to talk about textbooks. In the past 20 years or so there has been a positive change in the quality of textbooks. For the most part, information is better organized, identified, illustrated and described. They also tend to be easier to understand. They often have good illustrations, questions at the beginning or end of chapters, summaries and glossaries. On the other hand, there's far more information to learn than ever before! The vast amount of information in some textbooks can be overwhelming. The following advice will help you get past the psychological barrier some people are faced with when looking at all this information.

We will now bring all your skills together and allow you to do very well with books you need to absorb in the future. Take a textbook you need to read and casually glance over it, looking through the table of contents, the front and back covers, preface, and leaf through using your imagination. Tell yourself how much fun it's going to be to understand all the great information contained within it. Example: "I'm going to know all about string theory in a nonlinear universe!" Take a look through the first chapter, noting unusual type, getting familiar with charts and graphs, and any pictures or diagrams. Look at these with a childlike sense of wonder, excited that soon you will master all this knowledge.

Then start breaking that first chapter into manageable chunks, telling yourself how soon you'll be understanding everything you see. The idea is to convince your brain that there is nothing scary here. There's nothing here you can't handle with time and tools. Take a small section of two or three pages and preview it as you learned in chapter 7. Then read it. Then review it. Parrot and determine if you need further review. Once you have a strong idea of the information, take on the next couple of pages or so. Stay in control of how much you are absorbing. It is essential to build a good solid foundation of knowledge when starting a new area of study.

There are two different schools of thought on unknown vocabulary words. One school says to look through the text, try to spot any words that you do not know and learn their meaning before reading. The other school says you should try to figure them out when you come to them from their context. If you cannot, then decide whether it is worth looking them up. The first way makes for a smoother reading experience when you get to the reading stage (after previewing—see chapter 7); while the second requires you to stop the reading process and consider what to do. I suggest trying both and deciding which works best for you (for more on this, see the following section on learning vocabulary). You may want to look at the section with difficult vocabulary

LEARNING AND MEMORY   **241**

first. If your brain is all turned on, take advantage of that. Just make certain you are not simply avoiding Topic A by showing great interest in Topic B. Remember, first things first.

Think of learning as like eating a multicourse meal. You eat the meal one bite at a time. Cut, chew and swallow. Shoving all the food into your mouth at once isn't only uncouth, it's unproductive. The same is true for information. Your mind will reject too much knowledge at once, just as your stomach will do with too much food.

When you are reading your textbook, use the Info-Mapping™ method for taking notes; and use imagery and pictorial stories to remember facts (see page 192). Remember to avoid using highlighter pens—this just teaches your brain to be lazy.

The most important thing is to keep a positive attitude and smile as you look through your textbook. Those first impressions play a big part in determining how your brain will process and accept the information.

ASSIGNMENT

Take a new textbook that you need to read and use the bookmark technique (see chapter 7 on previewing) to preview it.

Remembering words: meanings and spellings

Vocabulary
Remembering vocabulary words does not have to be a difficult, painstaking process. There is a simple and

effective technique, which does not require a great deal of thinking or stress. All it requires is a bit of time and diligence. Once you have made certain preparations, the rest of the process is as easy as listening to music.

Choose up to 18 words you do not know. Write them down with their meaning and a word or two that mean the same thing (synonyms) or put them in a sentence.

Make an audio recording. Use a strong, clear voice. Speak with authority. No mistakes or long pauses, so practice saying them first.

Lie down (don't fall asleep!) or sit quietly by yourself and listen to the recording 12 times in a row. Use headphones if you have them. Repeat every night for one week; then get someone to test you. They can ask you the meanings of the words in random order.

If you miss any of these meanings, include them in your list of words for next week. If you missed two words, then you can have a maximum of 16 **new** words in your next recording.

Keep doing this for as long as you want to learn new words. You can use the same procedure for spelling (see below). However, do **not** learn vocabulary and spelling in the same recording.

S-p-e-l-l-i-n-g-s

The steps to follow are the same as for vocabulary, but to learn spellings, record yourself as you say the word in a clear, authoritative voice, then spell it out clearly, and say the word again. It is much easier to have the words and spellings written out in front of you as you record them.

Pause for a moment, and then do the next word. Again, the maximum number of words per recording is 18. If you are below the age of 10 or 11, your maximum number of words is 12. If you can handle more, then try bumping it up, but do **not** exceed 18 words at any age. The number of audio repetitions per evening, as with vocabulary, is 12.

REMEMBER: Do **not** mix spelling and vocabulary drills on the same recording. Leave some time between the two different drills.

SUMMARY

- Our attitude affects our beliefs and our abilities. Our brain works better when we believe we are good; and when we make learning fun!

- Use the Roman room technique to enhance your ability to recall lists.

- Remember the five keys to memory—movement, association, repetition, imagination and emotion (M.A.R.I.E.).

- Recorded repetition can effectively increase your vocabulary and improve your spelling ability.

14.

Focusing your mind

We have already seen how a key to learning is focus. This chapter looks at simple and effective ways to help you focus your mind and get completely absorbed in your reading, with outstanding results. It includes the exciting technique of enhanced focusing, which will offer you the chance to really let go!

As humans, we have an ability that takes us beyond any other living creature on the planet. We can **choose** to give our whole attention to one thing. Animals do this naturally. The lioness stalking the antelope is thinking of nothing else. One hundred percent of her attention is devoted to that antelope. However, she cannot bring that intense focus to anything beyond her instincts as related to survival. There is no freedom of choice; only to focus on survival skills.

Have you ever heard about people who devote their whole lives to one thing, becoming totally involved with one idea? What happens to the efforts of these people? Don't they usually come up with something new and amazing? Well, maybe not every time. However, every time someone comes up with something amazing, it is because they got very involved with that subject. They got very focused and absorbed and before you knew it they discovered something wonderful.

You can do the same thing with your reading! You can get very focused and absorbed into your reading and achieve amazing things.

Getting focused

The first step is to **decide** that you are going to absorb the information. Then visualize a clear mental picture of you knowing the information (see chapter 12). The next step is to get focused on the material by employing your senses. Your senses are how you interface with the world. Every bit of information you get comes through one or more of your senses. In the following assignment you are going to combine your senses with your imagination. You will be using your vision, hearing, olfactory and kinesthetic senses. The purpose of the assignment is to get focused by paying attention to what you are doing. This will help to shut out everything else so any distractions are minimized.

ASSIGNMENT

First, look at a piece of reading material, whether it's a book, journal or on a screen. You don't have to read it; just look at the shapes and colors on the page or screen. Now, visualize the words and pictures lifting off the page, going directly into your eyes and then up into your brain. Imagine a steady flow of information coming into you through your eyes.

Next, feel the book or paper. If it's a screen, simply turn your palms toward it. Imagine the words and pictures flowing from the page into your hands, moving up your arms and spreading all through your body. It's like dipping a paper towel into a colorful liquid. The liquid is absorbed into the material. Visualize all the words are being stored in your body and/or mind.

Now use your nose. Breathe in slowly and sense the words and pictures going right into your lungs. A few slow, deep breaths will do it. You can also feel the information spreading from your lungs to the rest of your body.

Finally, use your ears. As you begin to preview the material (see chapter 7), imagine the words coming into your ears like physical energy. Then speak the main words and thoughts from the text. Your mind will be more clear, relaxed and interested in the material. As you focus on the material to be absorbed, your attention is taken away from the distractions of your environment.

HINT: As is always the case, the clearer your reading area is, the easier it is to focus your mind. See page 251 for more on this.

Artificial interest

In chapter 13 I explained how getting interested is a matter of getting yourself into the right position to read. To take this further, you can generate artificial interest by getting into a position that suggests fascination. What you do is sit on the edge of your seat with your head forward; feet flat on the floor. Think about it! This is how you sit when you are hearing something amazing. Open your eyes wide and look focused and intent. Say to yourself that this is fascinating stuff. If you tell yourself that it is, it will soon become more so. Pretend that you are interested and soon you will be. This is because every time you have been highly interested in something in reality, your body has reacted this way. When you put yourself into a physical state of interest, your brain responds the same way it did before: with interest.

Pretending to be interested can lead to **being** interested.

Also, as you read, watching for answers to the magnetic questions (chapter 7, Who, What, When, Where, Why, How?), the game is really afoot and you begin to get tuned in. If nothing else, you will become interested in the process of learning that is taking place.

ASSIGNMENT

Take a piece of reading you would normally be very reluctant to do. Pick it up (or bring it up if on-screen) and declare how wonderful it will be to read this material. Say to yourself how much you're looking forward to it and can't wait to get started. Declare how thankful you are to have this in your life. Sit in a posture of excited fascination and smile as you dig in. Every few minutes remind yourself how lucky you are to have this and keep smiling. When finished, note the differences between this and other times you have tried to read such material.

The enemies of concentration

How you are getting on with your reading can be a good barometer for how you are taking care of yourself in general. Several factors, all fairly controllable, can contribute to a lack of concentration and focus. Let's take them one at a time.

Lack of sleep

The amount of sleep needed is different from person to person. Some people seem able to function quite well with only four or five hours of sleep per night. Others would be useless with only that amount and require eight to ten hours to function well. Teenagers need more sleep but many are unlikely to get it, with school and other activities. Studies show that the ideal time for most teenagers to sleep would be from about midnight to 10 in the morning. They are really waking up fully about 10:30 a.m. The school system does not help with this requirement. The best we can do until society changes if you are a teenager is to get to bed "early" and wake up in time to be ready for school.

On days when you have not had enough sleep, expect that your performance could be lower than usual. Taking this into account, you can compensate by doing extra previewing (see chapter 7). For example, you could combine key sentence previewing with name and number scan. If you are really tired but you must read, you may have to resort to reading aloud (while pointing).

ASSIGNMENT

Get to bed at a decent time tonight. Visualize yourself jumping out of bed in the morning energized and happy. Repeat for 21 days.

Poor nutrition

You are what you eat. Fresh fruit and vegetables provide the kind of nutrients that foster good mental performance. Be wary of "heavy" foods (such as too many carbohydrates) that give you a bloated feeling. Your body must make neurotransmitters from what you feed it. The best transmitters are made from whole, healthy foods high in amino acids. Highly processed foods are not good for concentration. Caffeine seems to give a temporary boost, but some studies show it to be detrimental to memory.

Your brain works using neurotransmitters such as acetylcholine and not having enough reduces mental performance. Acetylcholine-rich foods include peanuts, egg yolks, meat, fish, milk, wheat germ, cheese and vegetables (especially cauliflower, broccoli and cabbage). You also need protein, which is found in meat, fish, nuts and dairy foods. You will also want to make sure you're getting enough omega-3, which is found in oily fish, or take a good quality supplement. Brain-boosting vitamins include the B complex, as well as A, C and E (so you can ACE your exams). The minerals manganese, magnesium, calcium and potassium are also beneficial to brain function.

ASSIGNMENT

Eat a balanced diet with fruit, vegetables and drink loads of water for one week. How do you feel? Repeat.

Stress

Have you ever tried to accomplish something important while your head was swimming with worry? Stress can affect focus, memory and patience (among other things). If you are worried about something, trying to do some reading will give you a good indication of just how much it's affecting you. It's very easy to judge because you will either remember something or you will not. Remember, when you are learning SuperReading™, you must not be afraid of the truth. If you don't remember something that's important you want to know about it, not pretend that you did remember it. If you have uncomfortable thoughts running in your head, then you are probably stressed.

Experts tell us there is good stress and bad stress. That is fine. For our purposes, any stress which lowers our reading ability is bad stress. What can you do? There are two kinds of fixes: short term and long term. Long-term fixes address the root cause of the stress. They can be time consuming. However, if something is bothering you that much, it may be your mind begging you to deal with it. Short-term fixes get you to forget about your problem for a while. Hopefully that's long enough to get on with the business at hand. An exercise like alphabet animals (page 220) can be quite helpful to lighten your mood and replace bothersome imagery and emotions.

> **ASSIGNMENT**
>
> Run through an alphabet animals exercise next time you are feeling stressed and need to learn something. Look through page 220, pick an animal and have fun with it.

Busy environment

A clear work area fosters good concentration. If work that needs your attention is within view, your subconscious mind is aware of it and your attention may be divided. Best practice is to have as many things as possible out of your vision. Remember the old adage, "Out of sight, out of mind."

A to-do list is also helpful, as writing it down lets your mind know it can release the thoughts surrounding those items. It is important to have a safe place to keep your list. Your mind must be certain that once something is on the list, it is safely filed away and cannot be forgotten.

ASSIGNMENT
Start making to-do lists. Keep them safely.

Noise pollution

Words can catch our attention. Odd sounds from the environment around you can do the same. Some people are even bothered by rhythmic sounds. Here are some techniques that will help you to avoid being distracted:

Visualization (page 192)—see yourself absorbing information while surrounded by distractions. See a smile on your face.

Affirmation (page 198)—tell yourself how you are able to maintain focus in all conditions.

Finally, you can try **extreme focus**—consider that you might be distracted because your brain isn't challenged enough. You need to fill it with only one task; in this case, reading. Consider the following scenario. You just discovered a piece of paper that describes how to turn wood into gold. It's caught in a shredder and is slowly being pulled in. You only have about 20 seconds to read this piece of paper. Someone is asking if you would like to go to lunch later. There's an announcement on the public address system. Someone else just dropped some coins on the floor. Outside a dog is barking. Two people are arguing over who had the keys to the filing cabinet. Would you let any of that get in your way of reading that formula? No. You would be like a lion after its prey. You would completely ignore everyone and everything else. Isn't that right? You would be totally focused on that page.

The point is that if you are capable of concentrating in those conditions to discover how to turn wood into gold, you have the ability to focus under most conditions that are not threatening your immediate safety. So long as there's no fire you have the ability to concentrate and stay on task. What you need is the right motivation.

Quick focusing method

A development of the extreme focus technique described above is the quick focusing method, which will really help you to get your mind into a state of high concentration. In this method you read two (three, or four—it's up to you) books or pieces of writing at once, alternating between them every few seconds. You can experiment with how much time to spend on each book. After a minute or two (this varies), switch to the book you are more interested in. It can be one of the two or you can pick up a third book. Again, you can experiment to see what suits you best. As with all tools, what you prefer may vary from day to day.

Use as many different pieces for whatever length of time that you find solves your problem. For example, you could use four pieces for 15 seconds each. Or three pieces for 20 seconds each. Find the combination that works for you. You want to spend enough time to get the point but not so much time as you neglect the other material. It's all a matter of getting your mind into a state of high focus. Once you've achieved this state, reading the one text afterward will seem easy. The concept is to overwhelm the brain with information, then allow it to focus on only one thing.

ASSIGNMENT

Imagine that you must read a piece of text or someone will be hurt. Put two other pieces of writing in front of you and read the three in turn for about ten seconds each. By trying to keep all that information in mind, you will crowd out the other bothersome thoughts. Do this for a minute or two until you are really focused. Then push one away. Continue for another minute. Take the second away so now you only have the one you're really interested in. Your level of focus should be sufficiently high to overcome whatever was distracting you before. This is fighting fire with fire. Your brain wanted to multitask and you have used the problem as a solution.

Enhanced focusing technique

And now for the ultimate in focusing! When you use the enhanced focusing technique you will be able to let it all go and really have some fun. If all goes well you may find that you are more challenged than at any time in your life. There is one caveat: you should have been practicing pattern reading consistently well for at least a week (two weeks is better) before attempting the enhanced focusing technique.

The idea of this technique, which I use in the last class of my SuperReading™ courses, is to challenge your brain with a number of "handicaps" in order to make it work harder. Under ordinary circumstances your brain "feels" that it's capable of multitasking. It daydreams and runs various scenarios, conversations and theories, while you believe you are reading. It attends to sounds, noises and objects in your environment such as people, machinery, animals and anything else making a sound. The enhanced focusing technique can help you to overcome this "problem" and increase your level of focus and concentration.

Experiments suggest that you can show a person a page of text for less than a second, and under deep hypnosis they can recall everything on the page. This technique will mimic this phenomenon to a certain extent, but without the deep hypnosis. And when you actually read the book afterward, the information will seem familiar. You will catch on much more quickly than if you had not used this technique.

ASSIGNMENT

The first thing to do is find a book with large enough type that you do not have to squint to read, and preferably a title you have not read before, and which is not highly technical. Hardbacked books or large paperbacks are the best format. The type should not be too close to the gutter (the middle of the book when it is open). You will also need to have some music that you can play, preferably instrumental, although you may find that the extra challenge of words is OK. Some suggestions include:

Edgar Winter's "Frankenstein"
Vivaldi's *Four Seasons*
Hot Butter's "Popcorn"

Make a track list with one track playing after another. The order doesn't matter.

   While the surprise and timing of what happens in a class may be difficult to reproduce, I am going to use some creative techniques here to mimic what happens. Remember that, as with other advanced techniques, it takes practice and repetition to master. The first time you do this exercise it could take 20 to 30 minutes. With practice it should take you about a minute or so to get deeply focused, but please do this at a time when you will not be interrupted, including answering the telephone. The advantage of being focused on one thing at a time is that you are not getting interference from other thoughts, topics or previous annoyances.

NOTE: This exercise requires you to undertake a bit of role play. If you can imagine that the scenario is real it will work better for you.

Let's do it!

- Follow all instructions.
- Sit down at a desk or table, and clear the area in front of you of everything except the book you have chosen to work with.
- I want you to think of a person, alive, not with you, who you care for very much. Close your eyes and let this person come to mind. When you have the person's name, turn the page.

NEWS FLASH!

Crazed space aliens from another dimension have

invaded the Earth!

Among others, they have captured the person you were

just thinking of.

They are demanding that you get all the information that you

can out of the book in front of you . . .

In only 20 minutes!

If you don't, they will eject them into space—for an

unpleasant death.

You must not only be a super reader, you must be a

super hero!

Can you handle this challenge? Turn the page . . .

WHAT? I CAN'T *HEAR* YOU!

Can you handle this?

Along the way, there will be some challenges you have
to face.

- Every half-minute or so, you must blink your eyes
  three times.
- Between blink times you must tap your feet on the
  floor three times.
- As you begin you can turn on the music—loud!
- If you can get someone else to quickly flick the
  lights on and off and make random noises from
  time to time, it's even better.
- You will need to flip pages really quickly, about one
  page per second!
- **Do not** use your finger to read—it will be busy flipping pages. If you accidentally flip more than one
  page at a time, just keep going.

You will get another instruction on the next page.

Start your music, turn the page and start flipping the
pages for about five minutes while blinking and tapping.

REMEMBER, LIVES ARE AT STAKE!

Ready . . . start the music and turn the page.

- Before you begin flipping, rotate your book so the text is upside down.
- When you get to the other end of the book, start again and keep on flipping for five minutes. Go!

180 ⌄

Words words words words words words
words words words words words words
words words words words words words
words words words words words words
words words words words words words
words words words words words words
words words words words words words
words words words words words words
words words words words words words
words words words words words words
words words words words words words
words words words words words words
words words words words words words
words words words words words words
words words words words words words
words words words words words words
words words words words words words
words words words words words words

After five minutes, please pause the music.

So, how did that go? Rate your performance so far on a scale of zero to 10, with 10 being terrific and zero being rubbish.

Say your number out load.

If your score was anything less than 10, I have a question for you.

How dare you?

How dare you judge yourself so harshly?

How do you know you're not the best person to ever try this?

After all, when was the last time you read a book upside down, with feet tapping, eyes blinking and flipping pages as fast as you can?

Never? Then how can you judge?

If you gave yourself a mark of 10, terrific. Well done.

If not, be certain that you are a 10 and carry on with the music and everything else.

Focus and go for it as if lives depend on you.

Start the music up again.

Go for another five minutes with the book upside down, tapping and blinking, then stop.

Good, now rotate the book so it's right side up again.

Continue scanning one page per second and tapping and blinking for five more minutes.

Great. Now scan the pages every two seconds.

Continue tapping and blinking for four minutes.

Go!

Well done! Super!

Now scan up the left-side page and down the left-side page, up the right-side page and down the right-side page, then flip the page.

Take two seconds to go up; two seconds to go down.

Go for four minutes!

Now scan up for four seconds and down for four seconds.

Cut back on the tapping and blinking.

Go for four minutes!

Good.

Now find your natural pace in order to absorb the information. You should still be reading quite quickly, covering a page in between three and six seconds. The music can be turned down a bit, but still pushing you along.

Keep going for five to ten minutes.

Fantastic!

The crazed space aliens have been appeased!

Your loved one has been returned and their memory of this incident has been wiped.

They will have no recollection of what happened to them.

You, on the other hand, have a fairly good idea of what your book is about.

This assignment should have demonstrated that you are now capable of absorbing information at really high speeds. Think of it as another previewing tool for a book (see chapter 7 for more on previewing). With some practice you may find that in about 20 minutes you can come away with more information than a person who has spent two to three weeks living with the same book.

What you have been doing here is fooling your brain into hyperactivity. By getting you to "believe" it was a matter of life and death, you pooled resources not usually available. Next time you try this, simply imagine a similar situation, start with a book upside down for a minute or two and really get your brain up to speed. Once you're in high gear with the technique you can even switch materials after a minute or two and read something else. In other words, you do not have to turn the material you wish to read upside down. You can use other material to get yourself up to speed.

CAUTION: There is just one caution with this exercise: it does take up a bit of mental energy. Make sure you drink plenty of water afterward and remember to eat nutritiously.

The power break

Research shows that every few hours your body uses up its best neurotransmitters, the chemicals that allow your nervous system to function. As the supply is used up, the body must replace them with a less effective version. When that supply gets used up, it must replace that one with an even less effective one, and so on, all day long until we get what is known as our "second wind."

The problem is that these less effective transmitters cause wear and tear on our nervous system. By the end of the afternoon, our ability to concentrate and make good decisions declines. By the end of the work day we feel exhausted and spent. Even after a full night of sleep we still may not feel like we've caught up and that our cells have not got what they need to work at full capacity. In fact, what they need is a "power break" or "power nap" at some point during the day.

The solution is to take a 20-minute break to allow your body to manufacture more of the ideal neurotransmitters, which it cannot do when you are active. Only when you allow the body enough time to rest can it replenish the supply of these neurotransmitters. When it does, we feel refreshed, alert and calmly energized.

When is it the right time?

The body gives out clues as to when it needs a power break. They can be:

- feeling an itch
- yawning
- a leg "falling asleep"
- feeling hungry before a mealtime
- loss of concentration
- eyes not focusing well
- feeling stressed before an important deadline.

If you are feeling some or any of these, it could be time to take your power break.

What should I do?

Find a quiet place, away from noise or distractions. Sit comfortably or lie down. Do nothing. Don't try to think or not think. Your task is simply to sit for 20 minutes. For the first few minutes you may have many thoughts racing through your head. They will go away. Just sit. Your body knows what to do.

You could try smelling some vanilla before you begin as its aroma is very relaxing. Just a few gentle sniffs will do it.

WARNING: It is most important that you do not break for more than 20 minutes.

After about 25 minutes or so, your body may start to go into its sleep stages (delta brain waves), which will cause grogginess instead of alertness. Use a timer set for 20 minutes to ensure you break for the proper amount.

One or two power breaks per day will make a big difference in your productivity. You will have more energy all day long and wake up more refreshed in the mornings!

NOTE: As you slip into right-brain mode as you relax, intuitive insights may come to you. Keep a pen and paper or recorder with you. Simply write or record any interesting thoughts, put down the device and close your eyes again.

ASSIGNMENT

When your body shows signs that it might need one, take a power break for between 17 and 20 minutes. Set an alarm and just sit there. Repeat once or twice a day for 21 days. How do you feel? Remember to keep a notepad or voice recorder with you for when great ideas spring up.

Getting focused

1 **Decide** to absorb the material.

2 **See** a clear picture of it done.

3 **Look**—imagine absorbing through your eyes.

4 **Feel**—imagine taking information in through your hands.

5 **Nose**—imagine breathing in all the words and pictures.

6 **Ears**—imagine the words flowing right into your ears.

7 **Speak** the main words and thoughts.

Summary

- Decide what you want to achieve before you begin. As the famous writer Ralph Waldo Emerson said, "Once you make a decision, the universe conspires to make it happen."

- Artificial interest is often a lifesaver for people who have loads of dry, boring material to read.

While it is always helpful at any time, it is a real treasure for making the really dull stuff palatable.

- Defeating the enemies of concentration is so fundamental to good reading. While the basic techniques of this book go a long way, there is no reason to operate with strikes against you if it isn't necessary.

- Enhanced focusing is the ultimate focusing technique. Relax and enjoy it!

- The power break gets great reviews from people. What a simple way to save half your day. Try it for 21 days and look at the difference.

15.

Look to your future

Now you have come to the end of the main text of this book. What have you learned? In summary, loads!

In the first part of this book you discovered what SuperReading™ is all about and how it can help you (chapters 1 and 2). You have found out what kind of learner you are (chapter 3), how to test your reading effectiveness and monitor your progress (chapters 3 and 5). You know how important it is to reserve judgment with any new skill so you can embody that skill and fully benefit from it (chapter 4). You understand that you have to try it for at least 21 days or have 21 goes at it. You have discovered how to set reading goals and how to test yourself (chapters 4 and 5).

In the second part of this book, you learned the basic, essential techniques of SuperReading™. You discovered how to use hand pacing to point at what you are reading to keep your concentration (chapter 6). Then you learned how to P.RE.PA.R.E:

1 **Preview** the material so you know what's coming and improve recall (chapter 7)

2 **Read** (using your finger, of course!) (chapter 6)

3 **Parrot** to see if you've gained enough information (chapter 9)

4 If you are missing vital information, you then **review** to capture it (chapter 10)

5 **Embodying:** Do I want to put effort into storing this information in medium- or long-term memory (chapter 10)?

Other very important aspects of basic SuperReading™ include the Eye-Hop™, and you learned how to progress from processing one word at a time to taking on four- and five-word Eye-Hops™ (chapter 8). You will also have discovered some very useful techniques for reviewing and recall, including Info-Mapping™ (see chapters 10 and 13).

In the third part of this book, you looked at some very useful techniques to help you build on the basics of SuperReading™, from pattern reading (chapter 11), visualization and affirmation techniques (chapter 12), to methods for improving your memory, making learning fun and interactive (chapter 13), and focusing your mind (chapter 14).

You've now experienced SuperReading™. What's left to you now is knowledge. By investing some time each day in your personal development you can amass more useful information than you ever thought possible. The more you know, the more choices are available to you in your life.

From now on, schedule at least 30 minutes each day for personal reading to develop yourself. Choose a subject or topic that interests you and get a book on that subject. Using all your new skills, absorb the book and Info-Map™ it. This will take about eight hours. Get a second book on the same topic and do the same thing. This will take around six hours as much of the information will be similar. Add what you have learned to your Info-Map™. Get a third book on the topic. Look through the contents list and find out what's different. Read those sections and add the information to your Info-Map™. Get a fourth book . . . Do the same again with any new information, which by now is only around 10 to 20 percent of the content. This should take two hours at the most. Books five to ten should take you no more than an hour each to add to your Info-Map™. And so on. Then go to the Internet for any up-to-the-minute information to add to your Info-Map™. After a few months you will end up being an expert on the subject. If it's for a hobby, you will have reached a new level. If it's for your career, the sky's the limit. If knowledge is power, you have indeed become powerful.

The more you read the more you will know.
The more you know the more you can do.
The more you can do the more useful you are.
The more useful you are the more you are worth.
The more you are worth the higher your self-esteem.
The higher your self-esteem the greater can be your happiness.
The greater your happiness the more you may attain peace.
Having achieved peace, you can truly begin to help others.

Always read the best material you can, for it will determine your future.

Your reading coach, Ron.

Appendices

APPENDIX A

It's About Time

In chapter 1 you will have read of my quest, which I began in 1995, to find the solution to the problem of the apparent disappearance of time in a typical work day. I discovered that time disappeared into three areas: meetings, travel and reading. If you have been following the advice in this book you are probably well on the way to becoming a super reader, and the following strategies will save you even more time and help relieve or prevent stress.

> "If you don't have enough money or time, you must prioritize."
>
> JOHN EDMUND HAGGAI
> Christian motivational writer and speaker

On the telephone

Before you make a call, prioritize and **write down** the items you need to address. Tell the person when you call how many items you have to address, how long you believe it will take to go through them and confirm that they have the time to discuss them. Check the items off as you deal with them.

To finish: "Thank you, that's all I have for now. Is there anything you need? I'll call you [soon, Friday, next week, etc. . . .]. Thank you. Good-bye!"

ASSIGNMENT

For the next 21 days, keep a pad by the phone and write down the points you're going to cover with them for at least three people per day. Time your calls to check you are sticking to your estimated time for the conversation.

"To-do" list

Make a written list of the things you need to do today. Have a separate list for things to do tomorrow. Prioritize the top five items and commit yourself to doing them. Before you go to sleep, close your eyes and visualize them all completed. You will often wake up with great ideas to get them done more efficiently. If you can delegate or bin any items, do!

There is another good reason for having a written

"to-do" list. It can help you focus when you read. How? Do you ever have thoughts spinning endlessly round your head? Do you sometimes keep rehashing the same thing over and over, like when you can't get a tune out of your head? If so, a "to-do" list will help. I believe the swirling is the brain's attempt to not forget about it. The remedy is to convince your brain that it's OK to stop thinking about it by writing the item down and keeping it in a safe place, where your brain knows it cannot get away. Once that's done, your brain can relax in the confidence that the item will be handled and you will be able to focus on whatever you are doing, whether reading an article or anything else.

> ASSIGNMENT
> Try making "to-do" lists for 21 days or 21 times and see what happens. Your mind will learn to let the items go and focus on whatever you want it to.

Filing

File items according to subject or date. Cross-reference your list using a program such as MS Excel. Only keep what you really need. When you file things keep in mind that you should be able to find it again in 30 seconds or less. That will force you to be more logical and thoughtful and to think about finding something easily six months from now. Consider this: if you were away and had to ask someone else to find that paper for you, how could you ensure that it would be really easy to tell them how to find it in 30 seconds or less?

Backing up your computer files on a regular basis can save days of work. I back mine up every Friday onto an external drive. Once per quarter I back up the external drive onto writeable DVDs. Those should be kept in an entirely different place from your computer, like a safe deposit box, or with a trusted friend or relative.

Scheduling

Make appointments for any activity that takes at least 30 minutes. This is called scheduling. Make appointments with yourself and keep them. In the context of this book, make and keep appointments to do your reading practice every day (and to do the Eye-Hop™ exercises in chapter 8).

Only keep one calendar (a computer backup is OK). If you have two or more calendars you are inviting mayhem into your life. Eventually you will schedule an appointment that conflicts with one on the other calendar. Remember, "A man with a watch knows what time it is. A man with two watches is never sure."

Waiting

Always take something with you to do when you know you will have some waiting to do. Reading a book is a great idea. Or you can Info-Map™ projects (see chapter 10).

Write a note to a friend. Plan out your next day. Do your Eye-Hop™ exercises (see chapter 8). Review your goals. Write down some goals. Always turn waiting time into productive time.

> ASSIGNMENT
> Choose a book that you wish to absorb and put it in your briefcase, handbag, backpack, car or anywhere that makes sense to you. Do it now. Then pull it out and read it whenever you're in a line or waiting for something. Pretend that you are being paid by the minute to read that book.

Ideas

Keep a small notebook or voice recorder with you at all times. Whenever an idea comes to you record it. Later you can transfer your ideas into a more permanent file on your computer. Every couple of months glance through your ideas file. From time to time the moment will be right for one of your ideas. By having them fresh in your mind you will be ready when opportunity knocks.

They say "Opportunity only knocks once." I think there's more to it than that. I believe opportunity has a sense of humor. Not only does it only knock once, but sometimes it knocks very softly just to see if you're listening.

ASSIGNMENT

Keep an ideas file. Review them from time to time, such as monthly or quarterly. You will be surprised at what you've come up with. From time to time the timing will be right and you'll be able to capitalize on them.

SUMMARY

- Preparing for phone calls saves time while adding clarity.

- A to-do list not only keeps you more organized, it allows you to read with better focus.

- Good filing saves time and reduces stress.

- Proper scheduling saves time and reduces your stress levels.

- Turning waiting time into productive time makes your life easier.

- Recording our ideas leads to creative solutions and better focus.

APPENDIX B

Reading Tests and Answers

The tests

These are the remaining reading tests following on from Test 1 in chapter 5. For much more information on testing look back at chapter 5 to remind yourself. Have a timer (stopwatch) and a pen ready. Start your stopwatch; then begin to read. No note taking! Make sure you have a piece of paper in hand to cover up the questions so that you don't see them as you are reading.

Test 2: Antony van Leeuwenhoek

Antony van Leeuwenhoek was an unlikely scientist. A Dutch tradesman from a family of tradesmen, he was not wealthy and earned no university degrees. He only spoke Dutch.

Yet with skill, diligence and curiosity, free of the scientific dogma of the day, Leeuwenhoek made some of the most basic and important discoveries in biology. He discovered bacteria, parasitic microscopic organisms, sperm cells, blood cells, and microscopic nematodes and rotifers. His research opened up a new entire world of microscopic life to scientists.

Leeuwenhoek was born in 1632. His father was a basket maker and his mother's family were brewers. He started in business as a fabric merchant. He also worked as a surveyor and a wine assayer. Sometime during the 1660s, Antony van Leeuwenhoek learned to grind lenses. He made simple microscopes and began observing with them. He was inspired by Robert Hooke's illustrated book, *Micrographia*, which showed Hooke's own observations with the microscope.

Leeuwenhoek is known to have made over five hundred "microscopes," of which fewer than ten have survived. In basic design, probably all of Leeuwenhoek's instruments were simply powerful magnifying glasses, not compound microscopes of the type used today. Those were invented almost forty years before Leeuwenhoek was born. Sometimes he is referred to as "the inventor of the microscope." That would have been impossible.

Early compound microscopes were not practical for magnifying objects more than about twenty or thirty times. Leeuwenhoek's skill at grinding lenses allowed him to build microscopes that magnified over two hundred times, with clearer and brighter images than any of his colleagues could achieve. What helped was his curiosity to observe almost anything that could be placed under his lenses, and his care in describing what he saw. He hired an illustrator to make drawings of the things he saw, to accompany his written descriptions. Most of his descriptions of microorganisms are instantly recognizable.

In 1673, Leeuwenhoek began writing letters to the new Royal Society of London, describing what he had seen with his microscopes. His first letter had observations on the stings of bees. For the next fifty years he corresponded with the Royal Society. His letters, written in Dutch, were translated into Latin or English and printed in the Philosophical Transactions of the Royal Society. In 1680 he was elected a full member of the Royal Society.

His descriptions of tooth plaque are among the first observations of living bacteria ever recorded.

Note down your reading time; then answer the questions on the next page.

Time: _____

QUESTIONS FOR: Antony van Leeuwenhoek

1. In what year was Antony van Leeuwenhoek born?
2. What did van Leeuwenhoek's father do for a living?
3. Who wrote the book *Micrographia*?
4. What was invented almost forty years before van Leeuwenhoek was born?
5. What magnification did van Leeuwenhoek's microscopes achieve?
6. Whom did van Leeuwenhoek began writing letters to in 1673?
7. In what material did van Leeuwenhoek observe living bacteria?
8. How many microscopes did van Leeuwenhoek make?
9. In what two languages were van Leeuwenhoek's letters published?
10. Name one of the other careers van Leeuwenhoek had.

Now go back to the previous pages and read the article again.

Time yourself!

When you have finished answering go to page 301 and get the answers. Grade yourself.

Test 3: Conway Twitty

Conway Twitty was born Harold Lloyd Jenkins on 1 September 1933 in Friars Point, Mississippi. Jenkins was named by his great-uncle after his favorite silent movie actor, Harold Lloyd. The family moved to Arkansas when Jenkins was ten years old, and it was there that Jenkins formed his first singing group, the Phillips County Ramblers.

Two years later, he had his own local radio show every Saturday morning. Jenkins also practiced his second passion, baseball. He received an offer to play with the Philadelphia Phillies after high school, but he was drafted into the army, which effectively ended that dream.

Discharged from the army, Jenkins again pursued a music career. Upon hearing Elvis sing "Mystery Train," he began writing rock'n'roll songs. He worked with Sam Phillips, the owner and founder of Sun Studios in Memphis, to "get the right sound." None of those tracks were released.

Jenkins felt that his real name wasn't marketable, and he changed to his show-business name in 1957. Looking at a road map, he spotted Conway, Arkansas, and Twitty, Texas. He changed his professional name to "Conway Twitty."

Twitty's fortunes changed in 1958, while he was with MGM Records. His first Top 40 hit was "It's Only Make Believe." It was actually the B side of the single "I'll Try." Though it only made it to number two, it sold eight million copies. The record took nearly one year in all to reach and stay at the top spot of the charts in America and the UK. With his deep, resonant voice, some people thought it was Elvis recording under a different name. Twitty racked up nine Top 40 hits in his career.

Conway Twitty always wanted to record country music and in 1965 he switched genres. At first some country DJs refused to play his songs because he was well known as a rock'n'roll singer. His first top five country hit, "The Image of Me" came in July 1968, followed by his first number one country song, "Next in Line," that November.

In 1970, Conway recorded and released his biggest hit ever, "Hello Darlin'," which spent four weeks at the top of the country chart. His music has appeared in other media, including TV's *Family Guy* and the video game *Grand Theft Auto: San Andreas*. With two Grammys, Conway Twitty was inducted into the Country Music Hall of Fame in 1999.

Note down your reading time; then answer the questions on the opposite page.

Time: _____

QUESTIONS FOR: Conway Twitty

1. What was Conway Twitty's real name?
2. What was the name of his first singing group?
3. Twitty wanted to play baseball. What city offered him a contract?
4. What Elvis song inspired Twitty to begin writing rock'n'roll songs?
5. Twitty's first Top 40 song was "It's Only Make Believe." What song was the A side of the record?
6. How many copies did "It's Only Make Believe" sell?
7. What was the title of Twitty's first number one country song?
8. In what year was Twitty inducted into the Country Music Hall of Fame?
9. Who founded Sun Studios in Memphis?
10. What was Twitty's biggest country hit, which spent four weeks at number one?

Now go back to the previous pages and read the article again.

Time yourself!

When you have finished answering go to page 302 and get the answers. Grade yourself.

Test 4: David Livingstone

David Livingstone was a Scottish missionary and explorer of the Victorian era, now best remembered because of his meeting with Henry Morton Stanley, which gave rise to the popular quotation, "Dr. Livingstone, I presume?"

Livingstone was born in the village of Blantyre, South Lanarkshire, Scotland. He studied medicine and theology at the University of Glasgow. While working in London, Livingstone joined the London Missionary Society, becoming a minister.

From 1840 he worked in what is now Botswana, but was unable to make inroads into South Africa because of Boer opposition. He married fellow Scotsman Robert Moffat's daughter Mary in 1844, and she traveled with him for a brief time, despite being pregnant. She later returned to England with their children.

From 1852 to 1856, he explored the African interior, and was the first European to see Victoria Falls, which he named after Queen Victoria. Livingstone was one of the first Westerners to make a journey across Africa. The purpose of his journey was to open trade routes, while accumulating information about the African continent. Livingstone was a proponent of trade and missions to be established in central Africa. His motto, inscribed in the base of his statue at Victoria Falls, reads "Christianity, Commerce and Civilization."

He believed the key to achieving these goals was the navigation of the Zambezi River. He returned to Britain to raise funds, and to publish a book on his travels. He resigned from the missionary society. Livingstone returned to Africa as head of the government-funded "Zambezi Expedition," which was to examine the natural resources of southeastern Africa. The Zambezi River turned out to be completely unnavigable.

The expedition lasted six years. Livingstone was an inexperienced leader and had trouble managing a large-scale project. His wife, Mary, died on 29 April 1863 of dysentery, but Livingstone continued to explore, eventually returning home in 1864 after the government ordered the expedition recalled.

In March 1866, Livingstone returned to Africa to seek the source of the Nile. Livingstone was taken ill and completely lost contact with the outside world for six years. Henry Morton Stanley, sent by the *New York Herald* newspaper in 1869, found Livingstone on the shores of Lake Tanganyika in 1871. Stanley joined Livingstone, and together they continued exploring the north end of the Tanganyika.

Despite Stanley's urgings, Livingstone was determined not to leave Africa until he completed his mission. He died from malaria in 1873.

Note down your reading time; then answer the questions on the next page.

Time: _____

QUESTIONS FOR: David Livingstone

1. In what Scottish village was Livingstone born?
2. What subjects did Livingstone study at university?
3. Livingstone first worked in what part of Africa?
4. What was Mary Livingstone's maiden name?
5. Livingstone was the first European to see what African landmark?
6. The inscription on Livingstone's statue reads, "Christianity, Commerce and _____"?
7. Which river did Livingstone believe was paramount to his goals for Africa?
8. How long did the government-funded expedition last before being recalled?
9. What did David Livingstone die from?
10. What newspaper sent Stanley to find Livingstone?

Now go back to the previous pages and read the article again.

Time yourself!

When you have finished answering go to page 302 and get the answers. Grade yourself.

Test 5: William Morris

William Morris was one of the principal founders of the British Arts and Crafts Movement and is best known as a designer of wallpaper and patterned fabrics. He was a writer of poetry and fiction, and an early founder of the socialist movement in Britain.

The tragic conflict in Morris's life was his unfulfilled desire to create affordable—or even free—beautiful things for common people. The real-life result was always the creation of extremely expensive objects for the discerning few. In his utopian novel, *News from Nowhere,* everybody works for pleasure only, and beautifully handcrafted things are given away for free to those who appreciate them.

Morris was born in Walthamstow near London. His family was wealthy, and he went to Exeter College, Oxford, where he was influenced by John Ruskin. He met his wife, Jane Burden, a working-class woman whose pale skin and coppery hair were considered by Morris the epitome of beauty.

The artistic movement Morris and his friends made famous was the Pre-Raphaelite Brotherhood. They disfavored the rough industrial manufacture of decorative arts and architecture, and favored a return to hand-craftsmanship, raising craftsmen to the status of artists.

Morris left Oxford to join an architectural firm, but found himself drawn to the decorative arts. In 1861, he founded the firm of Morris, Marshall, Faulkner &

Company. Throughout his life he continued to work in his own firm, although it changed names. Its most famous incarnation was as Morris and Company. His designs are still sold today under licenses given to Sanderson & Sons and Liberty of London. In 1877 he founded the Society for the Protection of Ancient Buildings. His preservation work resulted indirectly in the founding of the British National Trust.

Morris and his daughter May were among Britain's first socialists, working with Eleanor Marx and Friedrich Engels to begin the socialist movement. In 1884 he organized the Socialist League.

Morris's book, *The Wood Between the Worlds,* is said to have influenced C. S. Lewis's Narnia series, while J. R. R. Tolkien was inspired by Morris's books *The House of the Wolfkings* and *The Roots of the Mountains.*

After the death of Tennyson in 1892, Morris was offered the Poet Laureateship, but declined. William Morris died in 1896 and was buried in the churchyard at Kelmscott village in Oxfordshire.

Note down your reading time; then answer the questions on the next page.

Time: _____

QUESTIONS FOR: William Morris

1. William Morris is best known as a designer of wallpaper and _____?
2. Morris's utopian novel was entitled _____?
3. Where did Morris go to college?
4. His wife's maiden name was _____?
5. The artistic movement he helped made famous was the Pre-Raphaelite _____?
6. In 1877 he founded the Society for the Protection of _____?
7. Name one person Morris worked with to begin the socialist movement in Britain.
8. What were Morris's daughters' names?
9. *The House of the Wolfkings* influenced what author?
10. Which Poet Laureate died in 1892?

Now go back to the previous pages and read the article again.

Time yourself!

When you have finished answering go to page 303 and get the answers. Grade yourself.

Test 6: Ezra Pound

Ezra Weston Loomis Pound was a poet, critic and intellectual. He was a major figure of the modernist movement in the first half of the twentieth century. He is generally considered the poet most responsible for defining and promoting a modernist aesthetic in poetry. In the early twentieth century, he opened a seminal exchange of work and ideas between British and American writers, and was famous for the generosity with which he advanced the work of such major contemporaries as Robert Frost, Marianne Moore, Ernest Hemingway and, especially, T. S. Eliot. Pound also had a profound influence on Irish writers William Butler Yeats and James Joyce.

His own significant contributions to poetry begin with his promotion of Imagism, a movement in poetry that derived its technique from classical Chinese and Japanese poetry, stressing clarity, precision and economy of language, and forgoing traditional rhyme and meter in order to, in Pound's words, "compose in the sequence of the musical phrase, not in the sequence of the metronome." His later work, for nearly fifty years, focused on the epic poem he entitled *The Cantos*.

Pound was born in America, where he attended several universities. In 1908 he moved to Europe, settling in London after spending a brief stint working as a tour guide in Gibraltar, and several months in Venice.

In the years before the First World War, Pound was

responsible for the appearance of Imagism and Vorticism. These two movements helped bring to notice the work of poets and artists such as James Joyce and Robert Frost.

Pound believed William Butler Yeats was the greatest living poet, and befriended him in England. Pound eventually became Yeats's secretary, and soon became interested in his occult beliefs. During the First World War, Pound and Yeats lived together at Stone Cottage in Sussex, England, studying Japanese, especially Noh plays. In 1914, Pound married artist Dorothy Shakespeare.

In 1920, Pound moved to Paris, where he worked among a circle of artists, musicians and writers who were revolutionizing the whole world of modern art. He was friends with Ernest Hemingway, whom Pound asked to teach him to box.

In 1924, Pound left Paris permanently and moved to Italy. During the Second World War, Pound created propaganda for the Axis, and later faced charges of treason in America. He spent twelve years in St. Elizabeth's mental hospital in Washington, DC. Upon release, he moved to Venice, where he is buried today.

Note down your reading time; then answer the questions on the next page.

Time: _____

QUESTIONS FOR: Ezra Pound

1. Which movement in poetry is derived from Chinese poetry?
2. Name two major contemporary poets whose work was advanced by Pound.
3. Pound worked for fifty years on what poem?
4. In what year did Pound move to Europe?
5. What was the name of Ezra Pound's wife?
6. What was the name of the place where Pound lived with Yeats?
7. Imagism stresses three qualities. Please name one.
8. Imagism and Vorticism helped to bring notice to two poets. Please name one.
9. In what Washington, DC, hospital did Pound spend twelve years?
10. Where did Pound work as a tour guide?

Now go back to the previous pages and read the article again.

Time yourself!

When you have finished answering go to page 303 and get the answers. Grade yourself.

Test 7: Ansel Adams

Ansel Easton Adams was an American photographer, known for his black and white photographs of California's Yosemite Valley.

Adams was the author of numerous books about photography, including his trilogy of technical instruction manuals: *The Camera, The Negative* and *The Print.*

He invented the zone system, a technique allowing photographers to translate the light they see into specific densities, giving them better control over finished photographs. Adams pioneered the idea of visualization of the finished print based upon the measured light values in the scene being photographed.

Adams was born in San Francisco. When he was four, he broke his nose on a garden wall in an aftershock from the 1906 San Francisco earthquake. His nose appeared crooked for the rest of his life.

He became interested in photography when his Aunt Mary gave him a copy of *In the Heart of the Sierras* while he was sick as a child. The photographs piqued his interest enough to persuade his parents to vacation in Yosemite National Park in 1916, where he was given a camera as a gift.

Adams disliked the uniformity of the education system and left school in 1915 to educate himself. He trained himself as a pianist, and alternated between a career as a photographer and a concert pianist. Photography won out, as did Yosemite, where he met his future wife, Virginia Best.

At the age of 17 Adams joined the Sierra Club, a group dedicated to preserving the natural world's wonders and resources. He remained a member throughout his lifetime and served as a director. Adams was an avid mountaineer and participated in the club's annual "high trips." It was at Half Dome in 1927 that he first found that he could make photographs that were, in his own words, ". . . an austere and blazing poetry of the real." Adams became an environmentalist, and his photographs are a record of what many of these national parks were like before human intervention. His work promoted many of the goals of the Sierra Club and brought environmental issues to light.

Adams was the recipient of three Guggenheim fellowships during his career. He was elected in 1966 a Fellow of the American Academy of Arts and Sciences. In 1980 Jimmy Carter awarded him the Presidential Medal of Freedom, the nation's highest civilian honor. The Minarets Wilderness in the Inyo National Forest was renamed the Ansel Adams Wilderness in 1984 in his honor.

Note down your reading time; then answer the questions on the next page.

Time: _____

QUESTIONS FOR: Ansel Adams

1. Name two of Adams's three instruction manuals.
2. What was the name of the technique Adams invented to help photographers translate light into densities?
3. On what did Adams break his nose when he was four years old?
4. In which national park did Adams's family holiday in 1916?
5. What was Adams's wife's name?
6. What group did Adams join at the age of 17?
7. Who awarded Adams the Presidential Medal of Freedom?
8. The Minarets Wilderness was in which national park?
9. In 1927, Adams photographed what natural feature?
10. How many Guggenheim Awards did Adams receive?

Now go back to the previous pages and read the article again.

Time yourself!

When you have finished answering go to page 304 and get the answers. Grade yourself.

The answers and scoring

Remember that you do not score your tests until you have completed both the test and the re-test.

Here's how to score your tests:

1 When you get an answer totally correct both in the test and the re-test, give yourself a score of 10.

2 Give yourself a zero when you get an answer wrong or leave it blank. Numerical answers must be totally correct or you score zero.

3 Score 5 for a partially correct answer. For example, if the correct answer is "Alexander Fleming," you get 5 points for "Fleming" and 10 points for "Alexander Fleming."

4 Add up your numbers—this gives you your comprehension score. For example, 70 points represents 70 percent comprehension.

5 Turn to Appendix D to calculate your Reading Effectiveness (R.E. score).

The first set of answers goes with Test 1 in chapter 5 on pages 65–7.

Test 1: George Stephenson

1 Wylam

2 Ten years

3 Blucher

4 Flanged

5 Gravity

6 Edward Pease

7 Locomotion

8 Experiment

9 Cuts or embankments or (stone) viaducts [need one only]

10 Rocket

Test 2: Antony van Leeuwenhoek

1 1632

2 Basket maker

3 Robert Hooke

4 Compound microscopes

5 Over 200 times

6 The Royal Society of London

7 Tooth plaque

8 Over 500

9 Latin and English

10 Fabric merchant or surveyor or wine assayer

302 SUPERREADING FOR SUCCESS

Test 3: Conway Twitty

1 Harold Lloyd Jenkins
2 The Phillips County Ramblers
3 Philadelphia
4 "Mystery Train"
5 "I'll Try"
6 Eight million
7 "Next In Line"
8 1999
9 Sam Phillips
10 "Hello Darlin'"

Test 4: David Livingstone

1 Blantyre
2 Medicine and theology
3 Botswana
4 Moffat
5 Victoria Falls
6 Civilization
7 The Zambezi
8 Six years
9 Malaria
10 *New York Herald*

Test 5: William Morris

1 Patterned fabrics
2 *News from Nowhere*
3 Exeter College, Oxford
4 Burden
5 Brotherhood
6 Ancient Buildings
7 Eleanor Marx or Friedrich Engels (surname OK)
8 May
9 Tolkien
10 Tennyson

Test 6: Ezra Pound

1 Imagism
2 Robert Frost, Marianne Moore, Ernest Hemingway or
   T. S. Eliot
3 *The Cantos*
4 1908
5 Dorothy Shakespeare
6 Stone Cottage
7 Clarity, or precision or economy of language
8 James Joyce or Robert Frost
9 St. Elizabeth's
10 Gibraltar

Test 7: Ansel Adams

1 *The Camera, The Negative* and *The Print*
2 The zone system
3 A garden wall
4 Yosemite
5 Virginia Best
6 The Sierra Club
7 Jimmy Carter
8 Inyo
9 Half Dome
10 Three

APPENDIX C

Calculating Your
Reading Speed

To calculate your reading speed, count the number of words on several full lines of your book to get an average. Multiply by the number of lines on a page. Depending on the type of book you are reading, the number of words per page is likely to fall somewhere between 150 and 400. Time yourself reading a page (or two) and see where the time and words per page meet on the following chart. This is your reading speed. For example, if you take 20 seconds to read a page with 300 words, your words per minute reading speed will be 900.

00.01 to 00.30 SECONDS

Time	150	175	200	225	250	275	300	325	350	375	400
00:01	9000	10500	12000	13500	15000	16500	18000	19200	21000	22500	24000
00:02	4500	5250	6000	6750	7500	8250	9000	9600	10500	11250	12000
00:03	3000	3500	4000	4500	5000	5500	6000	6400	7000	7500	8000
00:04	2250	2625	3000	3375	3750	4125	4500	4800	5250	5625	6000
00:05	1800	2100	2400	2700	3000	3300	3600	3840	4200	4500	4800
00:06	1500	1750	2000	2250	2500	2750	3000	3200	3500	3750	4000
00:07	1286	1500	1714	1929	2143	2357	2571	2743	3000	3214	3429
00:08	1125	1313	1500	1688	1875	2063	2250	2400	2625	2813	3000
00:09	1000	1167	1333	1500	1667	1833	2000	2133	2333	2500	2667
00:10	900	1050	1200	1350	1500	1650	1800	1920	2100	2250	2400
00:11	818	955	1091	1227	1364	1500	1636	1745	1909	2045	2182
00:12	750	875	1000	1125	1250	1375	1500	1600	1750	1875	2000
00:13	692	808	923	1038	1154	1269	1385	1477	1615	1731	1846
00:14	643	750	857	964	1071	1179	1286	1371	1500	1607	1714
00:15	600	700	800	900	1000	1100	1200	1280	1400	1500	1600
00:16	563	656	750	844	938	1031	1125	1200	1313	1406	1500
00:17	529	618	706	794	882	971	1059	1129	1235	1324	1412
00:18	500	583	667	750	833	917	1000	1067	1167	1250	1333
00:19	474	553	632	711	789	868	947	1011	1105	1184	1263
00:20	450	525	600	675	750	825	900	960	1050	1125	1200
00:21	429	500	571	643	714	786	857	914	1000	1071	1143
00:22	409	477	545	614	682	750	818	873	955	1023	1091
00:23	391	457	522	587	652	717	783	835	913	978	1043
00:24	375	438	500	563	625	688	750	800	875	938	1000
00:25	360	420	480	540	600	660	720	768	840	900	960
00:26	346	404	462	519	577	635	692	738	808	865	923
00:27	333	389	444	500	556	611	667	711	778	833	889
00:28	321	375	429	482	536	589	643	686	750	804	857
00:29	310	362	414	466	517	569	621	662	724	776	828
00:30	300	350	400	450	500	550	600	640	700	750	800

00.31 SECONDS to 1 MINUTE

Time	150	175	200	225	250	275	300	325	350	375	400
00:31	290	339	387	435	484	532	581	619	677	726	774
00:32	281	328	375	422	469	516	563	600	656	703	750
00:33	273	318	364	409	455	500	545	582	636	682	727
00:34	265	309	353	397	441	485	529	565	618	662	706
00:35	257	300	343	386	429	471	514	549	600	643	686
00:36	250	292	333	375	417	458	500	533	583	625	667
00:37	243	284	324	365	405	446	486	519	568	608	649
00:38	237	276	316	355	395	434	474	505	553	592	632
00:39	231	269	308	346	385	423	462	492	538	577	615
00:40	225	263	300	338	375	413	450	480	525	563	600
00:41	220	256	293	329	366	402	439	468	512	549	585
00:42	214	250	286	321	357	393	429	457	500	536	571
00:43	209	244	279	314	349	384	419	447	488	523	558
00:44	205	239	273	307	341	375	409	436	477	511	545
00:45	200	233	267	300	333	367	400	427	467	500	533
00:46	196	228	261	293	326	359	391	417	457	489	522
00:47	191	223	255	287	319	351	383	409	447	479	511
00:48	188	219	250	281	313	344	375	400	438	469	500
00:49	184	214	245	276	306	337	367	392	429	459	490
00:50	180	210	240	270	300	330	360	384	420	450	480
00:51	176	206	235	265	294	324	353	376	412	441	471
00:52	173	202	231	260	288	317	346	369	404	433	462
00:53	170	198	226	255	283	311	340	362	396	425	453
00:54	167	194	222	250	278	306	333	356	389	417	444
00:55	164	191	218	245	273	300	327	349	382	409	436
00:56	161	188	214	241	268	295	321	343	375	402	429
00:57	158	184	211	237	263	289	316	337	368	395	421
00:58	155	181	207	233	259	284	310	331	362	388	414
00:59	153	178	203	229	254	280	305	325	356	381	407
01:00	150	175	200	225	250	275	300	320	350	375	400

APPENDIX D

Reading Effectiveness (R.E.) Scores and Progress Graph

Once you have completed a test, look up your time in the left-hand column of the following tables (do this for both the test and then for the re-test). The number immediately to the right of your reading time is your words per minute (w.p.m.) score. Make a note of this.

The numbers across the top of the chart refer to your comprehension score. If, for example, you got five answers correct (5 x a score of 10), follow down the 50 column until it meets the row your time is on. The number where the column and row meet is your reading effectiveness (R.E.) score. The following charts are broken down into one-minute chunks to make it easier to quickly find your scores.

0:01 to 0:30 seconds

COMPREHENSION SCORE

Time	w.p.m.	10	20	30	40	50	60	70	80	90	100
00:01	24000	2400	4800	7200	9600	12000	14400	16800	19200	21600	24000
00:02	12000	1200	2400	3600	4800	6000	7200	8400	9600	10800	12000
00:03	8000	800	1600	2400	3200	4000	4800	5600	6400	7200	8000
00:04	6000	600	1200	1800	2400	3000	3600	4200	4800	5400	6000
00:05	4800	480	960	1440	1920	2400	2880	3360	3840	4320	4800
00:06	4000	400	800	1200	1600	2000	2400	2800	3200	3600	4000
00:07	3429	343	686	1029	1371	1714	2057	2400	2743	3086	3429
00:08	3000	300	600	900	1200	1500	1800	2100	2400	2700	3000
00:09	2667	267	533	800	1067	1333	1600	1867	2133	2400	2667
00:10	2400	240	480	720	960	1200	1440	1680	1920	2160	2400
00:11	2182	218	436	655	873	1091	1309	1527	1745	1964	2182
00:12	2000	200	400	600	800	1000	1200	1400	1600	1800	2000
00:13	1846	185	369	554	738	923	1108	1292	1477	1662	1846
00:14	1714	171	343	514	686	857	1029	1200	1371	1543	1714
00:15	1600	160	320	480	640	800	960	1120	1280	1440	1600
00:16	1500	150	300	450	600	750	900	1050	1200	1350	1500
00:17	1412	141	282	424	565	706	847	988	1129	1271	1412
00:18	1333	133	267	400	533	667	800	933	1067	1200	1333
00:19	1263	126	253	379	505	632	758	884	1011	1137	1263
00:20	1200	120	240	360	480	600	720	840	960	1080	1200
00:21	1143	114	229	343	457	571	686	800	914	1029	1143
00:22	1091	109	218	327	436	545	655	764	873	982	1091
00:23	1043	104	209	313	417	522	626	730	835	939	1043
00:24	1000	100	200	300	400	500	600	700	800	900	1000
00:25	960	96	192	288	384	480	576	672	768	864	960
00:26	923	92	185	277	369	462	554	646	738	831	923
00:27	889	89	178	267	356	444	533	622	711	800	889
00:28	857	86	171	257	343	429	514	600	686	771	857
00:29	828	83	166	248	331	414	497	579	662	745	828
00:30	800	80	160	240	320	400	480	560	640	720	800

0:31 to 1:00 minute

COMPREHENSION SCORE

Time w.p.m.	10	20	30	40	50	60	70	80	90	100
00:31 774	77	155	232	310	387	465	542	619	697	774
00:32 750	75	150	225	300	375	450	525	600	675	750
00:33 727	73	145	218	291	364	436	509	582	654	727
00:34 706	71	141	212	282	353	424	494	565	635	706
00:35 686	69	137	206	274	343	411	480	549	617	686
00:36 667	67	133	200	267	333	400	467	533	600	667
00:37 649	65	130	195	259	324	389	454	519	584	649
00:38 632	63	126	189	253	316	379	442	505	568	632
00:39 615	62	123	185	246	308	369	431	492	554	615
00:40 600	60	120	180	240	300	360	420	480	540	600
00:41 585	59	117	176	234	293	351	410	468	527	585
00:42 571	57	114	171	229	286	343	400	457	514	571
00:43 558	56	112	167	223	279	335	391	447	502	558
00:44 545	55	109	164	218	273	327	382	436	491	545
00:45 533	53	107	160	213	267	320	373	427	480	533
00:46 522	52	104	157	209	261	313	365	417	470	522
00:47 511	51	102	153	204	255	306	357	409	460	511
00:48 500	50	100	150	200	250	300	350	400	450	500
00:49 490	49	98	147	196	245	294	343	392	441	490
00:50 480	48	96	144	192	240	288	336	384	432	480
00:51 471	47	94	141	188	235	282	329	376	424	471
00:52 462	46	92	138	185	231	277	323	369	415	462
00:53 453	45	91	136	181	226	272	317	362	408	453
00:54 444	44	89	133	178	222	267	311	356	400	444
00:55 436	44	87	131	175	218	262	305	349	393	436
00:56 429	43	86	129	171	214	257	300	343	386	429
00:57 421	42	84	126	168	211	253	295	337	379	421
00:58 414	41	83	124	166	207	248	290	331	372	414
00:59 407	41	81	122	163	203	244	285	325	366	407
01:00 400	40	80	120	160	200	240	280	320	360	400

1:01 to 1:30 minutes

COMPREHENSION SCORE

Time	w.p.m.	10	20	30	40	50	60	70	80	90	100
01:01	393	39	79	118	157	197	236	275	315	354	393
01:02	387	39	77	116	155	194	232	271	310	348	387
01:03	381	38	76	114	152	190	229	267	305	343	381
01:04	375	38	75	113	150	188	225	263	300	338	375
01:05	369	37	74	111	148	185	222	258	295	332	369
01:06	364	36	73	109	145	182	218	255	291	327	364
01:07	358	36	72	107	143	179	215	251	287	322	358
01:08	353	35	71	106	141	176	212	247	282	318	353
01:09	348	35	70	104	139	174	209	243	278	313	348
01:10	343	34	69	103	137	171	206	240	274	309	343
01:11	338	34	68	101	135	169	203	237	270	304	338
01:12	333	33	67	100	133	167	200	233	267	300	333
01:13	329	33	66	99	132	164	197	230	263	296	329
01:14	324	32	65	97	130	162	195	227	259	292	324
01:15	320	32	64	96	128	160	192	224	256	288	320
01:16	316	32	63	95	126	158	189	221	253	284	316
01:17	312	31	62	94	125	156	187	218	249	281	312
01:18	308	31	62	92	123	154	185	215	246	277	308
01:19	304	30	61	91	122	152	182	213	243	273	304
01:20	300	30	60	90	120	150	180	210	240	270	300
01:21	296	30	59	89	119	148	178	207	237	267	296
01:22	293	29	59	88	117	146	176	205	234	263	293
01:23	289	29	58	87	116	145	173	202	231	260	289
01:24	286	29	57	86	114	143	171	200	229	257	286
01:25	282	28	56	85	113	141	169	198	226	254	282
01:26	279	28	56	84	112	140	167	195	223	251	279
01:27	276	28	55	83	110	138	166	193	221	248	276
01:28	273	27	55	82	109	136	164	191	218	245	273
01:29	270	27	54	81	108	135	162	189	216	243	270
01:30	267	27	53	80	107	133	160	187	213	240	267

1:31 to 2:00 minutes

COMPREHENSION SCORE

Time w.p.m.		10	20	30	40	50	60	70	80	90	100
01:31	264	26	53	79	106	132	158	185	211	238	264
01:32	261	26	52	78	104	130	157	183	209	235	261
01:33	258	26	52	77	103	129	155	181	206	232	258
01:34	255	26	51	77	102	128	153	179	204	230	255
01:35	253	25	51	76	101	126	152	177	202	227	253
01:36	250	25	50	75	100	125	150	175	200	225	250
01:37	247	25	49	74	99	124	148	173	198	222	247
01:38	245	24	49	74	98	122	147	171	196	220	245
01:39	242	24	48	73	97	121	145	170	194	218	242
01:40	240	24	48	72	96	120	144	168	192	216	240
01:41	238	24	48	71	95	119	143	166	190	214	238
01:42	235	24	47	71	94	118	141	165	188	212	235
01:43	233	23	47	70	93	117	140	163	186	210	233
01:44	231	23	46	69	92	115	138	162	185	208	231
01:45	229	23	46	69	91	114	137	160	183	206	229
01:46	226	23	45	68	91	113	136	158	181	204	226
01:47	224	22	45	67	90	112	134	157	179	202	224
01:48	222	22	44	67	89	111	133	156	178	200	222
01:49	220	22	44	66	88	110	132	154	176	198	220
01:50	218	22	44	65	87	109	131	153	175	196	218
1:51	216	22	43	65	86	108	130	151	173	195	216
1:52	214	21	43	64	86	107	129	150	171	193	214
1:53	212	21	42	64	85	106	127	149	170	191	212
1:54	211	21	42	63	84	105	126	147	168	189	211
1:55	209	21	42	63	83	104	125	146	167	188	209
1:56	207	21	41	62	83	103	124	145	166	186	207
1:57	205	21	41	62	82	103	123	144	164	185	205
1:58	203	20	41	61	81	102	122	142	162	183	203
1:59	202	20	40	61	81	101	121	141	161	182	202
2:00	200	20	40	60	80	100	120	140	160	180	200

2:01 to 2:30 minutes

COMPREHENSION SCORE

Time w.p.m.	10	20	30	40	50	60	70	80	90	100
02:01 198	20	40	60	79	99	119	139	159	179	198
02:02 197	20	39	59	79	98	118	138	157	177	197
02:03 195	20	39	59	78	98	117	137	156	176	195
02:04 194	19	39	58	77	97	116	135	155	174	194
02:05 192	19	38	58	77	96	115	134	154	173	192
02:06 190	19	38	57	76	95	114	133	152	171	190
02:07 189	19	38	57	76	94	113	132	151	170	189
02:08 188	19	38	56	75	94	113	131	150	169	188
02:09 186	19	37	56	74	93	112	130	149	167	186
02:10 185	19	37	55	74	92	111	129	148	166	185
02:11 183	18	37	55	73	92	110	128	147	165	183
02:12 182	18	36	55	73	91	109	127	145	164	182
02:13 180	18	36	54	72	90	108	126	144	162	180
02:14 179	18	36	54	72	90	107	125	143	161	179
02:15 178	18	36	53	71	89	107	124	142	160	178
02:16 176	18	35	53	71	88	106	124	141	159	176
02:17 175	18	35	53	70	88	105	123	140	158	175
02:18 174	17	35	52	70	87	104	122	139	157	174
02:19 173	17	35	52	69	86	104	121	138	156	173
02:20 171	17	34	51	69	86	103	120	137	154	171
02:21 170	17	34	51	68	85	102	119	136	153	170
02:22 169	17	34	51	68	85	101	118	135	152	169
02:23 168	17	34	50	67	84	101	117	134	151	168
02:24 167	17	33	50	67	83	100	117	133	150	167
02:25 166	17	33	50	66	83	99	116	132	149	166
02:26 164	16	33	49	66	82	99	115	132	148	164
02:27 163	16	33	49	65	82	98	114	131	147	163
02:28 162	16	32	49	65	81	97	113	130	146	162
02:29 161	16	32	48	64	81	97	113	129	145	161
02:30 160	16	32	48	64	80	96	112	128	144	160

2:31 to 3:00 minutes

COMPREHENSION SCORE

Time w.p.m.	10	20	30	40	50	60	70	80	90	100
02:31 159	16	32	48	64	79	95	111	127	143	159
02:32 158	16	32	47	63	79	95	111	126	142	158
02:33 157	16	31	47	63	78	94	110	125	141	157
02:34 156	16	31	47	62	78	94	109	125	140	156
02:35 155	16	31	46	62	77	93	108	124	139	155
02:36 154	15	31	46	62	77	92	108	123	138	154
02:37 153	15	31	46	61	76	92	107	122	138	153
02:38 152	15	30	46	61	76	91	106	122	137	152
02:39 151	15	30	45	60	75	91	106	121	136	151
02:40 150	15	30	45	60	75	90	105	120	135	150
02:41 149	15	30	45	60	75	89	104	119	134	149
02:42 148	15	30	44	59	74	89	104	118	133	148
02:43 147	15	29	44	59	74	88	103	118	133	147
02:44 146	15	29	44	59	73	88	102	117	132	146
02:45 145	15	29	44	58	73	87	102	116	131	145
02:46 145	14	29	43	58	72	87	101	116	130	145
02:47 144	14	29	43	57	72	86	101	115	129	144
02:48 143	14	29	43	57	71	86	100	114	129	143
02:49 142	14	28	43	57	71	85	99	114	128	142
02:50 141	14	28	42	56	71	85	99	113	127	141
02:51 140	14	28	42	56	70	84	98	112	126	140
02:52 140	14	28	42	56	70	84	98	112	126	140
02:53 139	14	28	42	55	69	83	97	111	125	139
02:54 138	14	28	41	55	69	83	97	110	124	138
02:55 137	14	27	41	55	69	82	96	110	123	137
02:56 136	14	27	41	55	68	82	95	109	123	136
02:57 136	14	27	41	54	68	81	95	108	122	136
02:58 135	14	27	40	54	67	81	94	108	121	135
02:59 134	13	27	40	54	67	80	94	107	121	134
03:00 133	13	27	40	53	67	80	93	107	120	133

3:01 to 3:30 minutes

COMPREHENSION SCORE

Time w.p.m.	10	20	30	40	50	60	70	80	90	100
03:01 133	13	27	40	53	66	80	93	106	119	133
03:02 132	13	26	40	53	66	79	92	105	119	132
03:03 131	13	26	39	52	66	79	92	105	118	131
03:04 130	13	26	39	52	65	78	91	104	117	130
03:05 130	13	26	39	52	65	78	91	104	117	130
03:06 129	13	26	39	52	65	77	90	103	116	129
03:07 128	13	26	38	51	64	77	90	103	116	128
03:08 128	13	26	38	51	64	77	89	102	115	128
03:09 127	13	25	38	51	63	76	89	102	114	127
03:10 126	13	25	38	51	63	76	88	101	114	126
03:11 126	13	25	38	50	63	75	88	101	113	126
03:12 125	13	25	38	50	63	75	88	100	113	125
03:13 124	12	25	37	50	62	75	87	99	112	124
03:14 124	12	25	37	49	62	74	87	99	111	124
03:15 123	12	25	37	49	62	74	86	98	111	123
03:16 122	12	24	37	49	61	73	86	98	110	122
03:17 122	12	24	37	49	61	73	85	97	110	122
03:18 121	12	24	36	48	61	73	85	97	109	121
03:19 121	12	24	36	48	60	72	84	96	109	121
03:20 120	12	24	36	48	60	72	84	96	108	120
03:21 119	12	24	36	48	60	72	84	96	107	119
03:22 119	12	24	36	48	59	71	83	95	107	119
03:23 118	12	24	35	47	59	71	83	95	106	118
03:24 118	12	24	35	47	59	71	82	94	106	118
03:25 117	12	23	35	47	59	70	82	94	105	117
03:26 117	12	23	35	47	58	70	82	93	105	117
03:27 116	12	23	35	46	58	70	81	93	104	116
03:28 115	12	23	35	46	58	69	81	92	104	115
03:29 115	12	23	34	46	57	69	80	92	103	115
03:30 114	11	23	34	46	57	69	80	91	102	114

3:31 to 4:00 minutes

COMPREHENSION SCORE

Time w.p.m.		10	20	30	40	50	60	70	80	90	100
03:31	114	11	23	34	45	57	68	80	91	102	114
03:32	113	11	23	34	45	57	68	79	91	102	113
03:33	113	11	23	34	45	56	68	79	90	102	113
03:34	112	11	22	34	45	56	67	79	90	101	112
03:35	112	11	22	33	45	56	67	78	89	100	112
03:36	111	11	22	33	44	56	67	78	89	100	111
03:37	111	11	22	33	44	55	66	77	88	100	111
03:38	110	11	22	33	44	55	66	77	88	99	110
03:39	110	11	22	33	44	55	66	77	88	99	110
03:40	109	11	22	33	44	55	65	76	87	98	109
03:41	109	11	22	33	43	54	65	76	87	98	109
03:42	108	11	22	32	43	54	65	76	86	97	108
03:43	108	11	22	32	43	54	65	75	86	97	108
03:44	107	11	21	32	43	54	64	75	86	96	107
03:45	107	11	21	32	43	53	64	75	86	96	107
03:46	106	11	21	32	42	53	64	74	85	95	106
03:47	106	11	21	32	42	53	63	74	85	95	106
03:48	105	11	21	32	42	53	63	74	84	95	105
3:49	105	10	21	31	42	52	63	73	84	94	105
3:50	104	10	21	31	42	52	62	73	83	94	104
3:51	104	10	21	31	42	52	62	73	83	94	104
3:52	103	10	21	31	41	52	62	72	83	93	103
3:53	103	10	21	31	41	52	62	72	82	93	103
3:54	103	10	21	31	41	51	62	72	82	93	103
3:55	102	10	20	31	41	51	61	71	82	92	102
3:56	102	10	20	31	41	51	61	71	81	92	102
3:57	101	10	20	30	41	51	61	71	81	91	101
3:58	101	10	20	30	40	50	61	71	81	91	101
3:59	100	10	20	30	40	50	60	70	80	90	100
4:00	100	10	20	30	40	50	60	70	80	90	100

4:01 to 4:30 minutes

COMPREHENSION SCORE

Time w.p.m.	10	20	30	40	50	60	70	80	90	100
04:01 100	10	20	30	40	50	60	70	80	90	100
04:02 99	10	20	30	40	50	60	69	79	89	99
04:03 99	10	20	30	40	49	59	69	79	89	99
04:04 98	10	20	30	39	49	59	69	79	89	98
04:05 98	10	20	29	39	49	59	69	78	88	98
04:06 98	10	20	29	39	49	59	68	78	88	98
04:07 97	10	19	29	39	49	58	68	78	87	97
04:08 97	10	19	29	39	48	58	68	77	87	97
04:09 96	10	19	29	39	48	58	67	77	87	96
04:10 96	10	19	29	38	48	58	67	77	86	96
04:11 96	10	19	29	38	48	57	67	76	86	96
04:12 95	10	19	29	38	48	57	67	76	86	95
04:13 95	9	19	28	38	47	57	66	76	85	95
04:14 94	9	19	28	38	47	57	66	76	85	94
04:15 94	9	19	28	38	47	56	66	75	85	94
04:16 94	9	19	28	38	47	56	66	75	84	94
04:17 93	9	19	28	37	47	56	65	75	84	93
04:18 93	9	19	28	37	47	56	65	74	84	93
04:19 93	9	19	28	37	46	56	65	74	83	93
04:20 92	9	18	28	37	46	55	65	74	83	92
04:21 92	9	18	28	37	46	55	64	74	83	92
04:22 92	9	18	27	37	46	55	64	73	82	92
04:23 91	9	18	27	37	46	55	64	73	82	91
04:24 91	9	18	27	36	45	55	64	73	82	91
04:25 91	9	18	27	36	45	54	63	72	82	91
04:26 90	9	18	27	36	45	54	63	72	81	90
04:27 90	9	18	27	36	45	54	63	72	81	90
04:28 90	9	18	27	36	45	54	63	72	81	90
04:29 89	9	18	27	36	45	54	62	71	80	89
04:30 89	9	18	27	36	44	53	62	71	80	89

4:31 to 5:00 minutes

COMPREHENSION SCORE

Time w.p.m.	10	20	30	40	50	60	70	80	90	100
04:31 89	9	18	27	35	44	53	62	71	80	89
04:32 88	9	18	26	35	44	53	62	71	79	88
04:33 88	9	18	26	35	44	53	62	70	79	88
04:34 88	9	18	26	35	44	53	61	70	79	88
04:35 87	9	17	26	35	44	52	61	70	78	87
04:36 87	9	17	26	35	43	52	61	70	78	87
04:37 87	9	17	26	35	43	52	61	69	78	87
04:38 86	9	17	26	35	43	52	60	69	78	86
04:39 86	9	17	26	34	43	52	60	69	77	86
04:40 86	9	17	26	34	43	51	60	69	77	86
04:41 85	9	17	26	34	43	51	60	68	77	85
04:42 85	9	17	26	34	43	51	60	68	77	85
04:43 85	8	17	25	34	42	51	59	68	76	85
04:44 85	8	17	25	34	42	51	59	68	76	85
04:45 84	8	17	25	34	42	51	59	67	76	84
04:46 84	8	17	25	34	42	50	59	67	76	84
04:47 84	8	17	25	33	42	50	59	67	76	84
04:48 83	8	17	25	33	42	50	58	67	75	83
04:49 83	8	17	25	33	42	50	58	66	75	83
04:50 83	8	17	25	33	41	50	58	66	74	83
04:51 82	8	16	25	33	41	49	58	66	74	82
04:52 82	8	16	25	33	41	49	58	66	74	82
04:53 82	8	16	25	33	41	49	57	66	74	82
04:54 82	8	16	24	33	41	49	57	65	73	82
04:55 81	8	16	24	33	41	49	57	65	73	81
04:56 81	8	16	24	32	41	49	57	65	73	81
04:57 81	8	16	24	32	40	48	57	65	73	81
04:58 81	8	16	24	32	40	48	56	64	72	81
04:59 80	8	16	24	32	40	48	56	64	72	80
05:00 80	8	16	24	32	40	48	56	64	72	80

5:05 to 7:30 minutes

COMPREHENSION SCORE

Time	w.p.m.	10	20	30	40	50	60	70	80	90	100
05:05	79	8	16	24	31	39	47	55	63	71	79
05:10	77	8	15	23	31	39	46	54	62	70	77
05:15	76	8	15	23	30	38	46	53	61	69	76
05:20	75	8	15	23	30	38	45	53	60	68	75
05:25	74	7	15	22	30	37	44	52	59	66	74
05:30	73	7	15	22	29	36	44	51	58	65	73
05:35	72	7	14	21	29	36	43	50	57	64	72
05:40	71	7	14	21	28	35	42	49	56	64	71
05:45	70	7	14	21	28	35	42	49	56	63	70
05:50	69	7	14	21	27	34	41	48	55	62	69
05:55	68	7	14	20	27	34	41	47	54	61	68
06:00	67	7	13	20	27	34	40	47	53	60	67
06:05	66	6	13	20	26	32	39	45	53	58	66
06:10	65	6	13	19	26	32	39	45	52	58	65
06:15	64	6	13	19	26	32	38	45	51	58	64
06:20	63	6	13	19	25	32	38	44	51	57	63
06:25	62	6	12	19	25	31	37	44	50	56	62
06:30	62	6	12	19	25	31	37	43	49	55	62
06:35	61	6	12	18	24	30	36	43	49	55	61
06:40	60	6	12	18	24	30	36	42	48	54	60
06:45	59	6	12	18	24	30	36	41	47	53	59
06:50	59	6	12	18	23	29	35	41	47	53	59
06:55	58	6	12	17	23	29	35	40	46	52	58
07:00	57	6	11	17	23	29	34	40	46	51	57
07:05	56	6	11	17	23	28	34	40	45	51	56
07:10	56	6	11	17	22	28	33	39	45	50	56
07:15	55	6	11	17	22	28	33	39	44	50	55
07:20	55	5	11	16	22	27	33	38	44	49	55
07:25	54	5	11	16	22	27	32	38	43	49	54
07:30	53	5	11	16	21	27	32	37	43	48	53

7:35 to 8:00 minutes

COMPREHENSION SCORE

Time w.p.m.		10	20	30	40	50	60	70	80	90	100
07:35	53	5	11	16	21	26	32	37	42	47	53
07:40	52	5	10	16	21	26	31	37	42	47	52
07:45	52	5	10	15	21	26	31	36	41	46	52
07:50	51	5	10	15	20	26	31	36	41	46	51
07:55	51	5	10	15	20	25	30	35	40	45	51
08:00	50	5	10	15	20	25	30	35	40	45	50

Reading Effectiveness Progress Graph

Example: Test 1 scores of 75 and 200

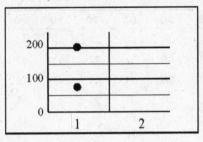

Fill in the following graph to keep track of your progress. Plot both your test R.E. score and your re-test R.E. score, one above the other. They should go above the Test Number. In other words, both your first scores from Test 1 should go above the 1.

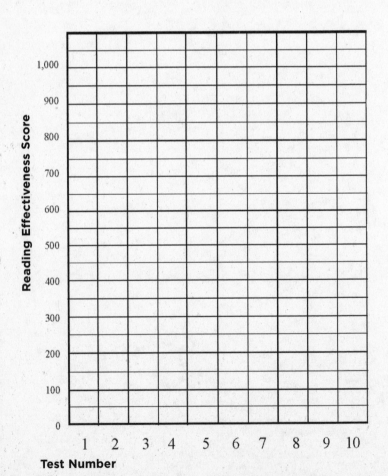

Index

INDEX

Entries in **bold** indicate charts and illustrations.

and speed visualization 198

computer screens 84–90, 91
color 88–9
and computer ergonomics 85
and font size 87
and hand pacing 85–6
using mouse pointers 84–5
position of 85
screen text 86–8

concentration *see* focus

conditioning, classical 83

confidence 225–7

Cooper, Ross 25

cynicism 35–6

delta waves 265

dialogue 103

digital audio 36, 40, 43

distraction
agents of 248–53, 267
"distracted reader syndrome" 23, 77–8

drifting off 23

dyslexia 24–5, 210–11

Einstein, Albert 29, 230

embodying 142–3, 147, 158, 160, 269

Emerson, Ralph Waldo 266

emotion, and memory 96–7, 145, 227, 229–30, 232

Engels, Friedrich 292

engineers 176, 180, 183

English as a second language
and affirmations 206
and Eye-Hop™ 125
and pattern reading 184–5
and previewing 106–8

and reading effectiveness testing 58–9
and vocabulary 107–8

enhanced focusing technique 189–90, 255–63, **260**, 267

environment, and focus 251–3

exaggeration 235

excellence 22–3

experience 45–6

eye dominance 20

eye muscles, damage to 19, 116

Eye-Hop™ 5–6, 10, 88, 115–33, 269
advanced 152, **153**
assignments 123, 132
booklets 118–20, **119**
and comprehension 120, 132, 133
and English as a second language 125
and hand pacing 116
and hop-drop 155
making your own 121–3
mastering 132
and page scan 154
and pattern reading 164, 173
and previewing 125
progress in 123–5
and reading effectiveness score 115
safety tips 121
samples 126–31
second word 165
skill levels 123–5, 126–31
technique 117–21

eyesight 245–6
ocular dominance 20

ABOUT THE AUTHOR

Ron Cole has been a trainer and personal coach since 1993. He learned his trade while living in Silicon Valley, California. He had been running a small advertising company for over five years when he signed up for a goal-setting course. What he learned there changed his life. Not only did his profitability nearly triple in six months, new ways of thinking and working infused themselves into his daily work.

After a few months Ron was asked to assist in teaching one of the courses. The thrill of helping people improve their lives was too much to resist. Over an 18-month period Ron dissolved his advertising agency and went into coaching full time. After another two years he started his own small company, offering coaching services.

Eventually his clients asked for help in managing their time better. This led to three areas of interest: travel, meetings and reading. For travel, Ron recommended books and audiotapes for continual learning. He taught best practice techniques for running smooth, productive meetings. Ron had experienced a speed reading course, but felt something more was needed for the kind of highly technical reading many of his clients were faced with. Over six months he experimented and came up with the basics for dealing effectively with large volumes of dense information.

After a year he got his first corporate client, Hewlett-Packard. He went from teaching a maximum of 8 people to 25! HP ordered three more courses and a new career began. Feedback from those professionals helped hone the course into a tight package which eventually included memory skills, visualization and motivational tools.

As the course spread to more companies, many of the delegates wanted their children to benefit from these skills. Some companies held family classes where adults and children took classes together. This was quite an experience for both groups. The adults were hard-pressed to keep up with the children, and the children benefited from seeing that adults were still interested in education. Eventually some schools brought the course in and the improvements were impressive. In one school the benefits were so profound that the students finished the entire curriculum in almost half the time!

At the writing of this book it's been 14 years, having taught thousands of people, from lawyers to teachers, engineers to bank managers and sales professionals to fourth-year students. They all now have one thing in common: reading is more fun, fast and productive.

Ron also teaches writing courses, NLP, goal achievement, negotiation, networking, visualization, remembering names, organization and presentation skills. His personal coaching skills include sales coaching and productivity.

If you would like more information about Ron's courses and coaching services, visit:

www.alchemy.name or
www.ofcourseihaveawebsite.com

If you enjoyed this book, visit

www.tarcherbooks.com

and sign up for Tarcher's e-newsletter to receive
special offers, giveaway promotions, and
information on hot upcoming releases.

TARCHER
PENGUIN

Great Lives Begin with Great Ideas

New at **www.tarcherbooks.com**
and **www.penguin.com/tarchertalks**:

Tarcher Talks, an online video series featuring
interviews with bestselling authors on everything from creativity and prosperity to 2012
and Freemasonry.

If you would like to place a bulk order
of this book, call 1-800-847-5515.

1/13 - WS